Kakuro Numbers Puzzles

By June Blanchard

Kakuro Numbers Puzzles

By June Blanchard

Atlanta, Georgia, 30305,
USA

Kakuro Numbers Puzzles

Solving Kakuro number puzzles is just as much of a challenge as word or crossword puzzles. The challenge of solving is in the clues.

Numbers one thru nine are used in the squares. Numbers are not repeated to solve the clue.

For example: No repeat numbers to solve clue in a puzzle.

Correct 5 + 3 = 8

4 + 2 = 6

3 + 1 = 4

For solving Kakuro numbers puzzles.

Use digits only 1 2 3 4 5 7 8 9

Below all **wrong** combinations of digits for solving Kakuro Numbers clues.

Wrong 8 4 + 4

Wrong 6 3 + 3

Wrong 4 2 + 2

Wrong 2 1 + 1

So, on and so on.

	35 ↓	17 ↓	8 ↓	7 ↓	19 ↓	12 ↓	9 ↓	4 ↓		18 ↓	6 ↓	13 ↓
43 →									13 ↓ 20 →			
12 →			9 ↓ 12 →				13 ↓	13 ↓ 12 →			27 ↓ 8 →	
14 →				18 ↓ 3 →		12 ↓ 24 →						18 ↓
2 →		16 ↓ 30 →								15 →		
11 →			9 ↓ 24 →						6 ↓	22 ↓ 15 →		
21 →					2 ↓	12 ↓		8 ↓ 14 →				
30 →							17 ↓ 14 →				14 ↓	13 ↓
	39 ↓ 3 →			22 ↓	11 ↓ 11 →				7 ↓ 14 →			
8 →		31 ↓	15 →			12 ↓ 37 →						
14 →			9 ↓ 23 →					25 ↓ 1 →		9 ↓	17 ↓	
24 →							12 ↓ 5 →		9 ↓ 11 →			13 ↓
17 →				16 ↓	11 ↓	37 →						
7 →			11 ↓ 5 →			6 ↓ 16 →				15 ↓	9 ↓ 5 →	
40 →									8 ↓ 16 →			
26 →					11 ↓	19 ↓	10 ↓	11 ↓ 10 →				18 ↓
1 →		7 ↓	13 ↓ 36 →							5 ↓	8 ↓ 7 →	
	3 ↓ 5 →			4 ↓ 18 →					2 ↓ 11 →			
31 →								15 →				

	7↓	23↓	16↓		14↓	10↓	9↓	10↓	9↓	2↓	14↓	11↓
17→				17↓ 42→								
36→							8↓ 5→			9↓ 11→		
	8↓ 2→		16↓ 19→					10↓ 9→				
17→						23↓	10↓ 8→		10↓ 5→		20↓	
15→					13↓ 23→							16↓
	45↓	15↓ 4→		8↓ 14→				15↓ 6→		30↓ 12→		
14→			17↓ 22→						33↓ 11→			
29→							6↓ 10→				1→	
24→						20↓ 20→					5↓ 8→	
2→		10↓ 3→			22↓ 9→			5↓ 15→				14↓
11→			22↓	10→			10↓ 20→				10↓ 3→	
11→				18→				27↓ 8→		18↓ 15→		
5→		22↓ 3→		18↓ 9→		2↓ 30→						
26→							21↓ 4→		6↓ 2→		18↓	7↓
33→						8↓ 33→						
	16↓ 5→		13↓ 7→		10↓ 16→				17↓ 10→			
7→		2↓ 27→						2↓ 8→		7→		8↓
17→				21→							8→	

	38 ↓		27 ↓	20 ↓	7 ↓	15 ↓	3 ↓	23 ↓	2 ↓		20 ↓	17 ↓
9 →		32 ↓ 33 →								10 ↓ 10 →		
32 →							5 ↓ 4 →		5 ↓ 13 →			
27 →					15 ↓	5 ↓ 32 →						
32 →							9 ↓ 12 →			40 ↓		
13 →				34 ↓ 7 →		23 ↓ 9 →		10 ↓	1 ↓ 1 →		15 ↓	
6 →			6 →		8 ↓ 3 →		12 ↓ 18 →					11 ↓
14 →			20 ↓ 27 →						1 ↓ 13 →			
	12 ↓	29 ↓ 8 →			16 ↓ 9 →			8 ↓ 9 →			21 ↓ 9 →	
40 →									32 ↓ 15 →			13 ↓
33 →						26 ↓	14 ↓	25 →				
12 →			16 →					2 ↓ 17 →				
	33 ↓ 8 →		19 ↓ 5 →		9 ↓ 22 →					20 ↓ 2 →		
8 →				10 ↓ 13 →				27 ↓ 8 →				4 ↓
7 →		24 ↓ 15 →					23 →				9 ↓ 4 →	
28 →					9 →		5 ↓ 28 →					8 ↓
21 →					8 ↓ 18 →				6 ↓ 2 →		13 ↓ 3 →	
5 →			1 ↓ 9 →			5 ↓ 9 →				7 ↓ 12 →		
12 →				6 →			5 →		13 →			

		31↓	23↓	12↓	2↓	12↓	11↓	4↓	10↓		15↓	32↓
	38→									12→		
	14→				22↓ 7→			16↓ 7→		19↓ 14→		
	39↓ 11→			2↓ 6→		8→			14↓ 16→			
19→						8↓	22↓ 28→					
10→				22↓ 30→							5↓ 6→	
14→			28→						6→			16↓
1→		21↓	14↓ 7→		1↓	2→				12↓	26↓ 7→	
18→						14↓ 4→		11↓	7↓ 9→			
25→					21↓ 6→		28→					
9→			17↓	11↓ 12→			7↓ 5→			7↓ 1→		8↓
44→									25↓ 18→			
	15↓ 22→						11↓	14↓ 7→		4↓ 11→		
2→		28↓ 1→		3↓		22↓ 32→						6↓
23→					5↓ 25→						11↓ 2→	
12→			15↓ 9→				20↓	14↓ 3→		8↓ 10→		
	6↓ 5→			15↓ 35→								10↓
16→					1↓	3↓ 14→			2↓ 5→		3↓ 3→	
36→								2→		10→		

	4 ↓	33 ↓	17 ↓	16 ↓	13 ↓	9 ↓				9 ↓		
30 →							2 ↓	1 ↓	9 →		20 ↓	
	7 ↓ 17 →					14 ↓ 3 →			7 ↓	9 ↓ 7 →		18 ↓
31 →							8 ↓	3 ↓ 25 →				
	45 ↓ 15 →			12 ↓	20 ↓ 14 →					5 ↓ 7 →		
14 →			19 ↓ 8 →			4 ↓ 6 →		18 ↓	15 ↓ 10 →			
25 →							27 ↓ 15 →				7 ↓ 5 →	
4 →		20 ↓ 16 →				14 ↓ 15 →				16 ↓ 7 →		15 ↓
18 →				26 →							11 ↓ 8 →	
18 →					21 ↓ 9 →			17 ↓	12 ↓ 18 →			
8 →				24 ↓ 31 →						5 ↓ 9 →		
6 →			6 ↓ 33 →								15 ↓	11 ↓
3 →		23 ↓ 19 →				24 ↓	22 ↓ 7 →		14 ↓	13 ↓ 8 →		
16 →			14 ↓ 21 →					3 ↓ 21 →				
	3 ↓ 9 →				28 →							16 ↓
15 →				9 ↓	8 ↓ 10 →			13 ↓ 6 →			11 ↓ 2 →	
	11 ↓ 39 →								10 ↓	11 ↓ 12 →		
7 →			3 ↓ 8 →		4 ↓ 9 →		27 →					
5 →		3 →		6 →			13 →					

	9↓	13↓		1↓	33↓	18↓	8↓	9↓	6↓	7↓	3↓	8↓
13→			13↓ 45→									
15→				10↓ 12→				17↓	3↓	5↓	4↓	23↓
	5↓ 24→						5↓ 27→					
5→		7↓	26↓ 32→						18↓	20↓	6↓ 7→	
	29↓ 23→					4↓	10↓	9↓ 30→				
8→		7↓ 5→		7↓	11↓ 22→						13↓ 2→	
26→						6→		40↓ 15→				21↓
3→		27↓ 6→				18↓ 7→			4↓	20↓ 11→		
14→				7↓ 9→			25→					
13→					11↓ 7→		5↓ 14→				13↓ 4→	
10→			20↓	7↓ 18→					17→			
	28↓ 32→						21↓ 9→		6→			
15→					26↓	7↓ 17→			17↓	8↓ 5→		20↓
3→		21↓ 40→									21↓ 5→	
19→				15↓ 8→		1→		9↓ 8→		12↓ 11→		
17→			13→			9↓ 7→			6↓ 14→			
6→			6↓ 20→				8↓ 17→					
13→				33→								

	20↓		14↓	4↓	12↓	13↓	14↓	14↓	8↓	9↓		19↓
8→		13↓ 42→									14↓ 7→	
16→				23↓ 25→					3↓	21↓ 11→		
20→					28↓ 8→		16↓	13↓ 21→				
10→			5↓ 15→			4↓ 8→			8↓ 7→			33↓
	24↓	19↓ 39→									17↓ 8→	
13→				20↓ 4→		7↓ 10→			9↓ 19→			
10→			16↓ 17→					37↓ 3→		20↓ 9→		
34→							3↓ 31→					
8→		13→			21↓	17↓ 7→			16↓ 7→		15↓ 4→	
5→		1→		36↓ 13→			14→					13↓
	17↓	4↓ 19→					6↓ 23→					
7→			5↓ 28→							22↓ 11→		
5→		20↓ 12→				8↓	16↓ 9→		9↓ 6→		6↓ 8→	
21→					18↓ 25→							20↓
10→			10↓ 24→					2↓ 17→			1→	
	9↓ 32→								15↓ 3→		3↓ 9→	
6→		9↓ 6→		3↓ 3→		2↓	6↓	4↓ 6→		7↓ 7→		
12→			36→								6→	

	8 ↓		27 ↓	8 ↓		13 ↓	13 ↓	9 ↓	6 ↓	13 ↓	5 ↓	3 ↓
8 →		8 ↓ 13 →			11 ↓ 42 →							
	15 ↓ 29 →								16 ↓ 5 →		22 ↓	18 ↓
5 →		22 ↓ 9 →		8 ↓ 4 →		13 ↓	1 ↓	11 ↓ 7 →		12 →		
45 →										26 ↓ 13 →		
9 →				19 ↓	3 ↓ 9 →		27 ↓ 9 →		11 ↓ 8 →			
	12 ↓ 4 →		19 ↓ 18 →					18 ↓ 22 →				3 ↓
27 →						17 ↓ 33 →						
17 →					24 ↓ 9 →				2 →		24 ↓ 2 →	
2 →		30 →							7 ↓ 9 →			18 ↓
	41 ↓	13 ↓ 3 →		5 ↓ 15 →			14 ↓	8 ↓ 7 →		9 ↓ 10 →		
8 →			25 ↓ 11 →			22 ↓ 12 →			21 ↓ 18 →			
11 →				11 ↓ 18 →				21 →				
24 →					2 ↓ 6 →			15 ↓ 9 →		8 ↓ 3 →		22 ↓
9 →		17 ↓ 40 →									14 ↓ 6 →	
16 →					8 ↓ 1 →		3 ↓ 13 →			12 ↓ 5 →		
4 →			3 ↓	12 ↓ 17 →				4 ↓	11 ↓ 16 →			
17 →					7 ↓	9 ↓	1 ↓ 20 →					
37 →								16 →				

	30 ↓			16 ↓	20 ↓	7 ↓	9 ↓	19 ↓	2 ↓	7 ↓	11 ↓	
4 →		20 ↓	1 ↓ 37 →									5 ↓
22 →							16 ↓ 3 →		13 ↓	13 ↓ 11 →		
10 →			11 ↓ 17 →			12 ↓ 25 →					7 ↓ 2 →	
13 →				34 →								2 ↓
20 →				8 ↓	21 ↓ 12 →			8 ↓ 3 →		17 ↓	17 ↓ 2 →	
3 →			11 ↓ 17 →				5 ↓ 5 →		17 ↓ 12 →			
		25 ↓ 8 →		18 ↓ 32 →								11 ↓
	21 ↓ 23 →					6 ↓	15 ↓	20 ↓ 26 →				
7 →			20 ↓ 26 →							13 ↓	10 ↓ 2 →	
20 →					19 ↓	26 ↓ 13 →			6 ↓ 14 →			
15 →				16 ↓ 36 →								34 ↓
8 →		18 ↓ 20 →					8 ↓	9 ↓	1 ↓	2 ↓	9 →	
	15 ↓ 45 →										15 ↓ 8 →	
7 →			18 →				17 ↓ 2 →		24 ↓	17 ↓ 15 →		
11 →			11 ↓	11 ↓ 8 →		13 ↓ 1 →		1 ↓ 22 →				
	1 ↓ 17 →				13 ↓ 22 →						15 ↓ 2 →	
31 →								19 →				
				16 →				21 →				

	36↓	29↓	5↓	22↓	1↓	11↓	7↓	9↓	7↓		23↓	17↓
45→										20↓ 15→		
19→					18↓ 14→				16↓ 20→			
9→			26↓ 12→				14↓	10↓ 16→				
27→						14↓ 25→						10↓
8→		14↓ 6→		6↓ 32→							20↓ 2→	
19→					25↓ 5→		17↓	8↓	6↓	11→		
45→										7↓ 4→		
13→			25↓	16↓ 9→		7↓ 8→		11↓	6↓ 12→			22↓
	41↓	10↓ 19→					8↓ 10→			15↓ 9→		
39→									28↓ 9→		5→	
21→					24↓ 8→			7↓ 10→			28↓ 7→	
16→				31↓ 8→		18↓	17↓ 24→					
11→			30↓ 24→							22↓ 5→		
8→		31→						15↓ 22→				6↓
1→		28→					19↓ 24→					
2→		3↓ 17→				4↓ 10→			9↓ 1→		3↓	9↓
19→					2↓ 39→							
	9→			12→					10→			

	8 ↓	8 ↓	14 ↓		18 ↓	4 ↓	14 ↓	21 ↓	10 ↓	9 ↓	10 ↓	1 ↓
13 →				13 ↓ 38 →								
6 →		16 →				22 ↓ 10 →				20 ↓ 7 →		11 ↓
		21 ↓ 32 →							7 ↓ 8 →			
	34 ↓ 1 →		15 ↓ 3 →		12 ↓ 14 →			4 ↓ 15 →			18 ↓ 2 →	
27 →							20 ↓ 4 →		18 →			
10 →				11 ↓ 13 →				24 ↓	20 ↓ 6 →			12 ↓
27 →						6 ↓ 11 →				9 ↓ 17 →		
15 →			20 ↓ 5 →		23 ↓ 25 →						10 ↓ 3 →	
7 →		35 ↓ 6 →		26 →						8 ↓ 1 →		
18 →				21 ↓ 9 →		30 →						15 ↓
	6 ↓ 20 →						18 ↓	9 ↓	8 ↓	22 ↓ 12 →		
24 →						14 ↓ 28 →						
	24 ↓ 2 →		19 ↓ 37 →								13 ↓ 5 →	
19 →				17 ↓	11 ↓ 8 →			22 ↓ 12 →				12 ↓
35 →							19 ↓ 5 →		5 ↓	4 ↓ 3 →		
24 →						4 ↓ 36 →						
3 →		4 ↓	7 ↓	5 ↓	19 →					2 ↓	7 ↓ 3 →	
24 →						9 →			9 →			

	37↓	1↓	23↓	7↓	13↓		9↓	12↓	16↓	7↓	8↓	7↓
18→						18↓ 36→						
8→		13↓ 8→		5↓ 11→			10↓ 7→			11↓	17↓ 5→	
18→					20↓ 33→							12↓
36→								13↓ 14→				
9→		18↓	3↓	18↓ 1→		9↓	14↓ 9→		18→			
39→									10↓	21↓	16↓ 3→	
23→						17↓ 6→		19→				5↓
	45↓ 2→		13↓ 9→		29↓ 9→		15↓	3↓ 16→				
17→				3↓ 18→					13↓ 8→			20↓
2→		12↓ 27→						7↓ 24→				
19→				21↓ 3→			27↓ 11→			10↓	1→	
10→			18↓ 16→			2↓ 6→		1↓ 5→			10↓ 3→	
9→		23↓ 23→							9↓ 20→			
26→						9→		26↓ 1→		12↓ 3→		1↓
16→					14↓	5↓ 24→						
9→				32→							8↓	
10→			6↓	7↓ 6→		3↓	9↓ 9→		2↓	5↓ 8→		9↓
		37→									9→	

	25↓	35↓	7↓	9↓	5↓	12↓		30↓	18↓	16↓	7↓	7↓
30→							7↓ 30→					
9→			18↓	20↓	15↓ 36→							
30→							9↓ 12→				8↓	13↓
33→						18↓ 11→			15→			
20→					6→		7↓ 1→		14↓	7↓	3↓ 3→	
21→					12↓ 32→							
	28↓	26↓	16↓	9↓ 5→				19↓ 8→			7↓	18↓
31→							17↓ 6→			14↓ 10→		
23→					6↓	27→					27↓ 2→	
18→						8↓ 11→			13↓ 15→			
18→				8↓	10↓ 11→			28↓ 21→				
	23↓ 5→		15↓ 20→				6↓ 8→			26↓ 7→		12↓
5→		31↓ 9→				4↓ 6→			2↓ 17→			
18→				2↓	24↓ 31→							
27→							2→		9→		18↓	11↓
11→				9↓ 3→		5↓	16↓ 6→		13↓ 16→			
11→			8↓ 28→							2↓ 8→		
	39→							22→				

	35 ↓	13 ↓	11 ↓	17 ↓	8 ↓	5 ↓	8 ↓	4 ↓			10 ↓	24 ↓
44 →									12 ↓	14 ↓ 17 →		
25 →						26 ↓	7 ↓	14 ↓ 17 →				
12 →				12 ↓	3 ↓ 26 →						12 ↓ 3 →	
9 →		3 ↓	15 ↓ 6 →				16 ↓ 7 →			17 ↓ 10 →		
23 →					13 ↓ 20 →				19 ↓ 18 →			
1 →		32 ↓ 26 →						20 ↓ 14 →				27 ↓
10 →			21 ↓	10 ↓ 34 →							17 ↓ 9 →	
	8 ↓ 17 →					23 ↓	10 →			19 ↓ 4 →		
22 →					28 ↓ 6 →		21 ↓ 25 →					
12 →				1 ↓ 21 →					18 ↓ 22 →			
	31 ↓ 28 →							22 ↓ 13 →			7 ↓ 4 →	
11 →			22 ↓	5 →		14 ↓ 13 →				12 ↓ 7 →		12 ↓
15 →				4 ↓ 27 →							12 ↓ 1 →	
3 →		24 ↓ 23 →					26 ↓ 25 →					
19 →					14 ↓ 15 →				14 ↓	19 ↓ 9 →		
14 →			10 ↓	9 ↓ 28 →								7 ↓
18 →						9 ↓ 9 →		8 ↓ 16 →			1 ↓ 1 →	
27 →					24 →				15 →			

	7↓	23↓	14↓	14↓	5↓	14↓	1↓	8↓	2↓		7↓	16↓
45→										11↓ 6→		
	7↓ 15→				24↓ 2→		10↓	15↓	7↓ 14→			
13→				6↓ 30→							5↓ 5→	
12→			9↓ 8→			10↓ 9→			22↓ 9→			21↓
	23↓	5↓ 7→		6↓ 17→			12↓ 16→			14↓	14↓ 9→	
29→								25↓ 18→				
6→		6↓	25↓	15↓ 9→		7↓ 34→						
25→					12↓ 5→		25↓ 20→					5↓
	8↓ 40→									19↓	8↓ 5→	
6→		30↓ 15→				30↓ 11→			17↓ 10→			17↓
12→					14↓ 13→			15↓ 25→				
	28↓ 4→			8↓ 32→							12↓ 5→	
4→			21↓ 21→				14↓ 9→		19↓	13↓ 10→		
14→				6↓ 19→				20↓ 16→				
26→					11↓ 33→							
16→				2→		5↓	6↓ 12→			5↓		12↓
6→		1↓ 1→		8↓ 17→					3↓ 5→		8↓ 9→	
25→						13→				11→		

	45↓	19↓	18↓		10↓	5↓	15↓	8↓	12↓	16↓		9↓
13→				9↓ 32→							5↓ 9→	
30→						23→						
18→					22↓	11↓ 2→		22↓ 10→				17↓
7→			10↓	14↓ 21→					6↓	24↓	17↓ 9→	
9→		30↓ 18→					11↓ 24→					
24→						15↓ 34→						
15→				10↓ 19→					7↓ 4→			4↓
11→			9↓ 16→					17↓ 14→			22↓ 4→	
19→					9↓	31↓	11↓ 14→					11↓
	36↓ 10→			10↓ 30→						11↓ 7→		
8→		26↓	12↓ 20→						3↓ 15→			
22→					14↓ 6→		13→				15↓ 8→	
39→								1↓	11↓	25↓ 8→		8↓
6→			13↓	13↓ 8→			19↓ 18→					
18→						11↓ 8→		13↓ 17→				
6→		15↓ 8→			11↓ 17→				6→		6↓	
39→									15→			9↓
	8→			13→					2→		9→	

	40 ↓	32 ↓	23 ↓	8 ↓	16 ↓	6 ↓	1 ↓	3 ↓		21 ↓	26 ↓	
38 →									3 ↓ 10 →			8 ↓
26 →						8 ↓	29 ↓	20 ↓ 24 →				
19 →				19 ↓	18 →				13 ↓ 7 →			9 ↓
29 →					6 ↓	8 ↓ 31 →						
3 →			24 ↓ 34 →							34 ↓	12 ↓ 3 →	
23 →					9 ↓	25 ↓ 3 →		7 ↓ 14 →				18 ↓
7 →		32 ↓ 26 →							22 ↓ 21 →			
13 →				20 ↓ 20 →				7 ↓ 10 →			5 ↓ 7 →	
	28 ↓ 18 →				4 ↓ 9 →		9 ↓ 19 →					
37 →								22 ↓ 20 →				
9 →			17 ↓ 5 →			13 ↓	9 ↓ 16 →				22 ↓	10 ↓
10 →					32 ↓ 28 →					11 →		
22 →				13 ↓ 12 →			25 ↓ 1 →		19 ↓	12 →		
7 →		30 ↓ 19 →				10 ↓ 9 →				9 →		
10 →			30 →							10 ↓	18 ↓	10 ↓
13 →			8 ↓ 18 →					11 ↓ 30 →				
	4 ↓ 23 →					7 ↓ 13 →			13 →			
15 →				12 →			5 →			4 →		

	12 ↓	2 ↓	3 ↓	31 ↓	5 ↓			26 ↓	8 ↓	16 ↓	13 ↓	15 ↓
26 →						7 ↓	4 ↓ 27 →					
2 →		11 ↓	4 →		4 ↓ 7 →				22 ↓ 19 →			
3 →			9 ↓ 12 →				14 ↓ 17 →				5 →	
	40 ↓ 24 →					15 ↓ 16 →					32 ↓ 3 →	
11 →			10 ↓ 5 →		16 ↓ 18 →					8 →		8 ↓
3 →		28 →						15 ↓ 4 →		6 →		
7 →		12 ↓ 6 →		28 ↓ 5 →			25 ↓ 4 →		6 ↓	26 ↓ 11 →		
5 →			6 ↓ 16 →			30 →						
20 →					14 ↓	10 ↓ 12 →			15 ↓ 10 →			16 ↓
33 →								21 →				
4 →		5 ↓	21 →					21 ↓ 9 →			15 ↓ 3 →	
7 →			4 ↓ 11 →			34 ↓	5 ↓ 9 →		3 ↓ 10 →			
	22 ↓	22 ↓ 4 →		5 ↓	1 ↓ 35 →							5 ↓
11 →			8 ↓ 13 →				15 ↓ 9 →			9 ↓ 9 →		
15 →					18 ↓ 14 →			7 ↓	16 ↓ 2 →		1 ↓ 2 →	
17 →				7 ↓ 31 →								7 ↓
4 →			8 ↓ 13 →					8 ↓ 10 →			9 ↓ 5 →	
	31 →						13 →			11 →		

	1 ↓	20 ↓	11 ↓	2 ↓	26 ↓		21 ↓	4 ↓	15 ↓	11 ↓	10 ↓	10 ↓
18 →						14 ↓ 34 →						
	13 →			20 ↓ 20 →				1 ↓ 20 →				
	33 ↓ 8 →		31 ↓ 25 →							1 →		11 ↓
33 →						5 ↓	13 ↓	27 ↓		10 ↓	3 →	
8 →		7 →			21 ↓ 9 →				16 ↓ 4 →		21 ↓ 2 →	
6 →		21 ↓ 16 →				13 ↓ 34 →						
10 →				27 →						8 ↓ 8 →		
16 →				12 →			11 ↓ 22 →					
15 →				18 ↓ 2 →		13 ↓ 8 →			19 ↓	25 ↓	12 ↓	8 ↓
	7 ↓ 6 →		20 ↓ 22 →					27 →				
22 →					20 ↓ 6 →			4 ↓ 17 →				
	27 ↓	18 ↓ 19 →					12 ↓ 15 →					9 ↓
28 →						9 →		28 ↓ 8 →			25 ↓ 4 →	
16 →				10 ↓ 2 →		2 ↓ 13 →				1 ↓ 11 →		
10 →			9 ↓ 9 →				8 ↓ 8 →		3 ↓ 8 →			11 ↓
5 →		12 ↓ 11 →			11 ↓	8 ↓ 10 →				17 ↓ 12 →		
18 →				7 ↓ 17 →					2 ↓ 15 →			
29 →								15 →				

	6↓	30↓	13↓		14↓	15↓	9↓	4↓	17↓		6↓	13↓
10→				16↓ 22→						10↓ 11→		
37→								10↓ 17→				
	15↓ 5→		18↓ 12→				3↓ 17→				2↓	
20→					2↓	7↓ 8→				28↓ 2→		11↓
36→									11↓ 5→		8→	
5→		23↓ 5→		31↓	11↓ 3→		8↓	17↓ 9→			7↓ 2→	
	7↓ 7→		11↓ 10→			11↓ 34→						
23→							18↓ 12→					19↓
24→					2↓ 22→					29↓	4↓ 7→	
	28↓ 8→		24↓ 7→			19↓ 12→			4↓ 12→			
9→		11↓ 13→			9↓ 11→			6↓ 9→			22↓ 5→	
13→				13↓ 16→					12↓ 17→			
35→							19↓	19↓ 12→				
1→		12↓ 8→				20↓ 28→						23↓
22→					14↓ 16→				3↓ 6→		13↓ 4→	
	4→		10↓	6↓ 19→						7↓ 9→		
	4↓ 28→							1↓	21→			
13→				8→		9→					9→	

	5 ↓	22 ↓	15 ↓	14 ↓		7 ↓	1 ↓	21 ↓	16 ↓	13 ↓	2 ↓	12 ↓
13 →					5 ↓ 32 →							
	32 ↓ 25 →						16 ↓ 19 →				8 ↓ 9 →	
22 →						26 ↓ 8 →			14 ↓ 9 →			12 ↓
14 →			35 ↓	16 ↓	8 ↓ 9 →			4 ↓ 4 →		16 ↓ 5 →		
8 →		38 →									12 ↓ 4 →	
9 →		16 →			16 →			6 ↓ 27 →				
4 →		36 ↓ 10 →			14 ↓ 1 →		10 ↓ 4 →		14 ↓	9 ↓ 1 →		8 ↓
	22 ↓ 11 →			19 ↓ 44 →								
36 →								6 →			28 ↓ 1 →	
27 →							8 ↓	18 ↓ 5 →		9 ↓ 3 →		
19 →					9 ↓	8 ↓ 11 →			13 ↓ 12 →			9 ↓
	6 →		33 ↓	17 →			11 ↓ 23 →					
	21 ↓ 13 →			13 ↓		19 →				21 ↓ 4 →		7 ↓
16 →					28 ↓	15 ↓ 32 →						
27 →								7 ↓	3 ↓ 4 →		20 ↓ 1 →	
6 →		3 ↓ 20 →					13 ↓ 17 →					
12 →				8 →		6 ↓ 9 →			17 →			5 ↓
12 →				22 →						11 →		

	41 ↓	24 ↓	21 ↓	6 ↓	2 ↓	13 ↓		18 ↓	18 ↓		4 ↓	
27 →							23 ↓ 7 →			4 →		19 ↓
20 →					24 ↓ 15 →					1 ↓	9 →	
20 →				27 ↓ 32 →							11 ↓ 4 →	
6 →			12 ↓ 10 →			17 →				22 ↓ 7 →		
26 →						15 ↓ 7 →			18 ↓ 15 →			
1 →		18 ↓ 14 →					7 ↓	18 →				
20 →					13 ↓ 15 →			15 ↓ 5 →			21 ↓	10 ↓
10 →			17 ↓ 12 →				8 ↓ 28 →					
	45 ↓ 13 →			9 ↓ 4 →		7 →			16 ↓ 15 →			
28 →						24 ↓ 7 →		13 ↓ 2 →		6 ↓ 7 →		
17 →					3 →		9 ↓ 14 →					25 ↓
7 →			29 ↓		9 ↓ 20 →					13 ↓	5 ↓ 2 →	
1 →		6 ↓ 5 →		9 ↓ 26 →					23 ↓ 15 →			
24 →					9 ↓ 7 →			19 ↓ 18 →				
2 →		15 ↓ 22 →					8 ↓ 8 →				13 ↓ 8 →	
20 →						6 ↓ 15 →				10 ↓ 10 →		
11 →				5 ↓	4 ↓ 34 →							4 ↓
27 →							5 →		9 →			

		34 ↓	13 ↓	3 ↓	1 ↓	24 ↓		30 ↓	10 ↓	10 ↓	1 ↓	8 ↓
	39 ↓ 23 →						13 ↓ 23 →					
12 →				9 ↓	25 →							15 ↓
24 →					18 ↓ 14 →					31 ↓	19 ↓ 9 →	
15 →			5 ↓	18 ↓ 24 →					29 ↓ 16 →			
34 →							9 ↓ 15 →					
7 →		21 ↓	20 ↓ 8 →			11 ↓ 7 →		10 →				4 ↓
39 →								23 ↓ 24 →				
20 →				10 ↓	13 ↓ 5 →		21 ↓ 22 →				24 ↓	
24 →						13 →				3 →		17 ↓
	20 ↓	25 ↓ 7 →				14 ↓ 21 →				17 ↓ 11 →		
16 →			16 ↓ 7 →		16 ↓ 12 →				16 ↓ 19 →			
17 →				12 ↓ 17 →				25 ↓ 10 →				
30 →							10 ↓ 19 →				25 ↓ 7 →	
23 →					3 ↓	19 ↓ 13 →				5 →		14 ↓
1 →			14 ↓ 27 →							3 ↓ 8 →		
	11 ↓	11 ↓ 8 →		3 ↓	10 ↓ 2 →		7 ↓ 9 →		8 ↓ 14 →			
32 →								9 ↓ 7 →		4 ↓ 8 →		
15 →				13 →			21 →					

	7 ↓	12 ↓	17 ↓	12 ↓	5 ↓	1 ↓	17 ↓		16 ↓	3 ↓	9 ↓	35 ↓
33 →								7 ↓ 14 →				
	40 ↓ 14 →					19 →				17 ↓ 13 →		
13 →				12 ↓		12 ↓	7 ↓	11 ↓ 9 →			9 →	
20 →					14 ↓ 34 →						4 ↓ 6 →	
1 →		3 ↓	22 ↓ 12 →				11 ↓ 3 →		7 ↓ 14 →			
42 →								25 ↓ 5 →			7 ↓	
8 →		2 →		28 ↓ 2 →		11 ↓ 11 →				25 ↓ 6 →		25 ↓
6 →		25 ↓ 12 →			4 ↓ 19 →				9 ↓ 16 →			
28 →							22 ↓ 20 →				2 ↓ 5 →	
	31 ↓ 9 →		16 ↓ 8 →		29 ↓	14 ↓ 10 →			20 ↓ 16 →			
35 →								14 ↓ 13 →			10 ↓ 3 →	
13 →				38 →								3 ↓
18 →				5 ↓ 9 →		18 ↓ 6 →				18 ↓ 8 →		
10 →			15 →				10 ↓ 20 →					14 ↓
9 →		6 ↓	12 ↓	11 ↓ 12 →				14 ↓	5 ↓ 7 →		8 →	
	7 ↓ 18 →				13 ↓ 21 →						13 ↓ 6 →	
19 →						7 ↓ 14 →				4 →		7 ↓
		3 →		16 →			1 →			16 →		

	31↓	16↓	19↓	8↓		12↓	30↓	14↓		17↓	15↓	4↓
20→					16↓ 14→				18→			
15→				14↓ 19→					18↓ 7→			1↓
30→						20↓ 32→						
3→		19↓ 28→						9↓ 8→		5↓ 1→		15↓
15→			18↓	14↓	18↓ 24→						5→	
29→							10↓ 6→			1↓	20↓ 2→	
	13↓ 30→							22↓	2↓ 11→			
7→		31↓ 14→				11→				12↓ 5→		10↓
13→				13↓			13↓ 3→		16↓ 9→			
10→			7→		7↓	5↓ 35→						
	28↓ 5→		17↓ 32→								21↓	6↓
21→						22↓ 16→				22↓ 12→		
16→				11↓	12↓ 3→		4↓		29↓ 12→			
13→			21↓ 21→					5↓ 18→				
5→		15↓ 12→					10↓ 17→					
14→					11↓ 10→			8↓ 8→			10↓	
12→				5↓ 39→								9↓
30→						14→				13→		

	6 ↓	12 ↓		16 ↓	5 ↓	2 ↓	24 ↓	20 ↓	13 ↓		5 ↓	27 ↓
15 →			11 ↓ 27 →							11 ↓ 9 →		
	21 ↓ 15 →					21 ↓ 28 →					2 ↓ 8 →	
14 →					21 ↓ 17 →				9 ↓ 14 →			
3 →		30 ↓	2 ↓ 20 →				16 ↓	4 ↓ 3 →			9 ↓ 6 →	
14 →				17 ↓ 29 →						12 ↓ 2 →		9 ↓
9 →			17 →					9 ↓ 26 →				
	9 ↓ 5 →		18 ↓ 7 →			24 ↓ 13 →			16 ↓ 3 →			16 ↓
29 →							7 →				14 ↓ 8 →	
17 →					24 ↓ 9 →		12 ↓	11 ↓ 8 →		9 ↓ 16 →		
	3 ↓ 10 →			27 ↓ 36 →								
2 →		14 ↓ 27 →							18 ↓ 1 →		6 ↓	18 ↓
10 →			20 ↓ 10 →			10 ↓ 9 →		18 ↓ 2 →		1 ↓ 14 →		
	24 ↓ 27 →						11 →				23 ↓ 9 →	
8 →		16 ↓ 7 →			19 ↓ 6 →		19 ↓ 6 →			5 →		
28 →						13 ↓ 20 →				15 ↓ 9 →		13 ↓
12 →				13 ↓ 24 →					14 ↓ 24 →			
5 →		6 ↓ 26 →						9 ↓ 18 →				
13 →			10 →				19 →					

	34↓	8↓	16↓		9↓	13↓	9↓	8↓		30↓	16↓	14↓
18→				17↓ 19→					22↓ 22→			
2→		16↓ 28→						5↓ 20→				
18→					6↓ 4→		15↓ 19→					
29→						13↓ 1→		8↓ 12→			5↓	17↓
7→			13↓	18↓	11↓ 37→							
5→		22↓ 28→						21↓	21↓ 6→		17↓ 6→	
30→						2↓ 22→				5↓ 5→		
	39↓ 9→		15↓ 11→				11↓ 15→					25↓
13→					17↓	13↓ 12→				9↓ 13→		
11→				27↓ 23→					13↓ 15→			
39→							11↓	5↓ 17→			22↓ 2→	
3→		14↓	5↓ 27→							17↓ 7→		
19→						15↓ 4→		15↓	15↓ 20→			
7→			17↓ 2→		8↓ 30→							5↓
34→							25→					
	10↓ 8→			5→		10↓	7↓ 10→			10↓		9↓
6→		8↓ 7→		5↓	10→			1↓	3↓ 6→		6↓ 2→	
20→					7→		21→					

	30 ↓	2 ↓	8 ↓	8 ↓	20 ↓	11 ↓	6 ↓		13 ↓	12 ↓	15 ↓	
41 →								20 ↓ 11 →				16 ↓
2 →		4 ↓	24 ↓ 8 →				26 ↓ 31 →					
16 →				8 ↓ 26 →						30 ↓	11 ↓ 2 →	
6 →		20 ↓ 19 →				9 ↓ 11 →			11 →			
20 →					9 ↓ 17 →				15 →			
33 →								14 ↓	8 ↓ 10 →			30 ↓
	24 ↓ 2 →		14 ↓	23 ↓	9 ↓	4 ↓	12 ↓ 14 →				5 →	
43 →									24 ↓ 9 →		7 →	
6 →		14 →				7 ↓ 9 →		6 ↓ 9 →			23 ↓ 9 →	
3 →		18 ↓ 7 →			14 ↓ 2 →		11 ↓ 10 →			4 →		
32 →								5 ↓ 5 →		22 ↓ 10 →		
	26 ↓ 6 →		9 →			16 ↓ 34 →						
6 →			16 ↓	15 ↓ 8 →			19 ↓ 3 →		14 ↓ 8 →			12 ↓
17 →					7 ↓ 15 →			5 ↓ 8 →			3 →	
9 →		15 ↓ 44 →									9 ↓ 5 →	
33 →						9 ↓ 5 →		14 ↓ 1 →		11 ↓ 11 →		
9 →			3 ↓	8 ↓	1 ↓ 5 →		7 ↓ 21 →					8 ↓
	30 →								8 →		8 →	

	45 ↓	17 ↓	11 ↓	3 ↓	2 ↓	6 ↓		19 ↓	10 ↓	4 ↓	17 ↓	
28 →							1 ↓ 28 →					8 ↓
11 →				24 ↓	22 ↓ 11 →					12 ↓ 14 →		
7 →			14 ↓ 17 →			5 ↓	8 ↓ 8 →		12 ↓ 12 →			9 ↓
2 →		36 ↓ 18 →						9 →			26 ↓ 9 →	
24 →						27 ↓ 7 →		16 ↓ 1 →		1 →		19 ↓
22 →					9 ↓ 1 →		12 ↓ 14 →			6 ↓ 15 →		
19 →				13 ↓ 22 →					16 ↓ 17 →			
14 →			26 ↓ 31 →							8 →		
28 →					14 ↓ 4 →		8 ↓	14 ↓ 5 →		5 ↓ 8 →		
	45 →										26 ↓ 2 →	
	6 ↓ 15 →					2 ↓	10 ↓ 5 →			31 ↓ 7 →		13 ↓
5 →		5 →		7 ↓	4 ↓ 11 →				11 →			
1 →		13 →				14 ↓ 1 →		8 ↓	7 →			
	15 ↓	21 ↓	6 ↓ 4 →		15 ↓ 18 →				19 ↓ 24 →			
11 →				6 ↓ 15 →			2 ↓ 23 →					7 ↓
17 →			10 ↓ 10 →			13 ↓ 2 →		13 ↓ 6 →			6 ↓ 7 →	
12 →					5 ↓ 6 →		23 →					3 ↓
14 →				12 →			8 →				3 →	

	41 ↓		7 ↓	13 ↓	14 ↓	8 ↓	16 ↓	8 ↓	7 ↓	5 ↓		8 ↓
5 →		9 ↓ 44 →									18 ↓ 8 →	
5 →			15 ↓ 15 →					6 ↓ 1 →		3 ↓ 2 →		28 ↓
26 →						12 ↓ 14 →			20 ↓ 10 →			
2 →		6 ↓ 9 →			20 ↓ 1 →			22 →				
20 →				14 ↓ 11 →			12 ↓	5 ↓ 7 →		16 ↓ 15 →		
6 →		6 ↓	20 ↓ 37 →								23 ↓ 6 →	
39 →								8 ↓	2 ↓ 16 →			
1 →		8 ↓ 5 →		17 ↓ 4 →		17 ↓	6 ↓ 7 →			24 ↓ 1 →		7 ↓
	33 ↓ 18 →				20 ↓ 8 →				36 ↓ 17 →			
35 →								6 ↓ 16 →				
2 →		30 ↓	2 ↓	4 ↓ 13 →			8 ↓ 16 →					15 ↓
23 →						30 ↓ 23 →					27 ↓ 4 →	
9 →			14 ↓ 14 →					1 ↓ 7 →		3 ↓ 10 →		
12 →					15 ↓ 7 →		24 ↓ 22 →					
15 →				15 →				5 ↓ 9 →		16 ↓ 8 →		22 ↓
13 →				19 →					10 ↓ 18 →			
	7 ↓ 11 →			8 ↓ 18 →				8 ↓ 10 →			5 ↓ 8 →	
7 →			14 →			24 →				14 →		

Solutions

	35 ↓	17 ↓	8 ↓	7 ↓	19 ↓	12 ↓	9 ↓	4 ↓		18 ↓	6 ↓	13 ↓
43 →	5	7	8	6	1	3	9	4	13 ↓ 20 →	9	6	5
12 →	3	9	9 ↓ 12 →	1	2	9	13 ↓	13 ↓ 12 →	8	4	27 ↓ 8 →	8
14 →	6	1	7	18 ↓ 3 →	3	12 ↓ 24 →	2	7	1	5	9	18 ↓
2 →	2	16 ↓ 30 →	2	1	9	5	3	6	4	15 →	8	7
11 →	4	7	9 ↓ 24 →	5	4	7	8		6 ↓	22 ↓ 15 →	6	9
21 →	7	5	6	3	2 ↓	12 ↓		8 ↓ 14 →	1	7	4	2
30 →	8	3	1	9	2	7	17 ↓ 14 →	1	5	8	14 ↓	13 ↓
	39 ↓ 3 →	1	2	22 ↓	11 ↓ 11 →	5	2	4	7 ↓ 14 →	3	5	6
8 →	8	31 ↓	15 →	7	8	12 ↓ 37 →	8	3	6	4	9	7
14 →	5	9	9 ↓ 23 →	6	2	8	7	25 ↓ 1 →	1	9 ↓	17 ↓	
24 →	2	3	5	9	1	4	12 ↓ 5 →	5	9 ↓ 11 →	3	8	13 ↓
17 →	7	6	4	16 ↓	11 ↓	37 →	4	3	8	6	9	7
7 →	3	4	11 ↓ 5 →	1	4	6 ↓ 16 →	6	9	1	15 ↓	9 ↓ 5 →	5
40 →	4	1	9	3	7	6	2	8	8 ↓ 16 →	8	7	1
26 →	9	8	2	7	11 ↓	19 ↓	10 ↓	11 ↓ 10 →	1	7	2	18 ↓
1 →	1	7 ↓	13 ↓ 36 →	5	3	8	9	4	7	5 ↓	8 ↓ 7 →	7
	3 ↓ 5 →	1	4	4 ↓ 18 →	6	4	1	7	2 ↓ 11 →	4	5	2
31 →	3	6	9	4	2	7		15 →	2	1	3	9

	7 ↓	23 ↓	16 ↓		14 ↓	10 ↓	9 ↓	10 ↓	9 ↓	2 ↓	14 ↓	11 ↓
17 →	3	5	9	17 ↓ 42 →	4	5	9	7	1	2	6	8
36 →	4	9	7	8	5	3	8 ↓ 5 →	3	2	9 ↓ 11 →	8	3
	8 ↓ 2 →	2	16 ↓ 19 →	6	3	2	8	10 ↓ 9 →	6	3		
17 →	5	6	3	1	2	23 ↓	10 ↓ 8 →	8	10 ↓ 5 →	5	20 ↓	
15 →	3	1	9	2	13 ↓ 23 →	7	3	2	4	1	6	16 ↓
	45 ↓	15 ↓ 4 →	4	8 ↓ 14 →	4	9	1	15 ↓ 6 →	6	30 ↓ 12 →	9	3
14 →	6	8	17 ↓ 22 →	2	5	1	6	8	33 ↓ 11 →	2	5	4
29 →	7	2	8	5	1	6	6 ↓ 10 →	4	1	5	1 →	1
24 →	9	5	6	1	3	20 ↓ 20 →	1	3	7	9	5 ↓ 8 →	8
2 →	2	10 ↓ 3 →	3		22 ↓ 9 →	4	5	5 ↓ 15 →	2	8	5	14 ↓
11 →	3	8	22 ↓	10 →	3	7	10 ↓ 20 →	5	9	6	10 ↓ 3 →	3
11 →	1	2	8	18 →	2	9	7	27 ↓ 8 →	8	18 ↓ 15 →	6	9
5 →	5	22 ↓ 3 →	3	18 ↓ 9 →	9	2 ↓ 30 →	3	8	6	7	4	2
26 →	4	8	5	6	1	2	21 ↓ 4 →	4	6 ↓ 2 →	2	18 ↓	7 ↓
33 →	8	9	6	3	7	8 ↓ 33 →	1	9	6	4	8	5
	16 ↓ 5 →	5	13 ↓ 7 →	7	10 ↓ 16 →	3	7	6	17 ↓ 10 →	5	3	2
7 →	7	2 ↓ 27 →	7	2	6	4	8	2 ↓ 8 →	8	7 →	7	8 ↓
17 →	9	2	6	21 →	4	1	5	2	9		8 →	8

	38↓		27↓	20↓	7↓	15↓	3↓	23↓	2↓		20↓	17↓
9→	9	32↓ 33→	7	5	1	6	3	9	2	10↓ 10→	7	3
32→	2	3	4	8	6	9	5↓ 4→	4	5↓ 13→	3	4	6
27→	7	5	9	6	15↓	5↓ 32→	5	2	1	7	9	8
32→	3	9	6	1	8	5	9↓ 12→	8	4	40↓		
13→	4	8	1	34↓ 7→	7	23↓ 9→	9	10↓	1↓ 1→	1	15↓	
6→	5	1	6→	6	8↓ 3→	3	12↓ 18→	3	1	6	8	11↓
14→	8	6	20↓ 27→	2	8	9	1	7	1↓ 13→	4	7	2
	12↓	29↓ 8→	7	1	16↓ 9→	5	4	8↓ 9→	1	8	21↓ 9→	9
40→	2	1	4	9	3	6	7	8	32↓ 15→	9	6	13↓
33→	7	6	9	3	8	26↓	14↓	25→	3	5	8	9
12→	3	9	16→	8	5	2	1	2↓ 17→	5	7	1	4
	33↓ 8→	8	19↓ 5→	5	9↓ 22→	4	7	2	9	20↓ 2→	2	
8→	1	5	2	10↓ 13→	4	3	6	27↓ 8→	1	3	4	4↓
7→	7	24↓ 15→	6	3	5	1	23→	9	6	8	9↓ 4→	4
28→	8	9	7	4	9→	9	5↓ 28→	4	8	7	9	8↓
21→	9	7	4	1	8↓ 18→	7	3	8	6↓ 2→	2	13↓ 3→	3
5→	2	3	1↓ 9→	2	7	5↓ 9→	2	1	6	7↓ 12→	8	4
12→	6	5	1	6→	1	5	5→	5	13→	7	5	1

		31 ↓	23 ↓	12 ↓	2 ↓	12 ↓	11 ↓	4 ↓	10 ↓		15 ↓	32 ↓
	38 →	6	5	9	2	8	1	4	3	12 →	3	9
	14 →	7	4	3	22 ↓ 7 →	4	3	16 ↓ 7 →	7	19 ↓ 14 →	9	5
	39 ↓ 11 →	8	3	2 ↓ 6 →	6	8 →	7	1	14 ↓ 16 →	7	1	8
19 →	3	4	9	2	1	8 ↓	22 ↓ 28 →	5	8	9	2	4
10 →	7	1	2	22 ↓ 30 →	8	3	7	4	6	2	5 ↓ 6 →	6
14 →	9	5	28 →	1	7	5	9	6	6 →	1	5	16 ↓
1 →	1	21 ↓	14 ↓ 7 →	7	1 ↓	2 →	2			12 ↓	26 ↓ 7 →	7
18 →	4	2	5	6	1	14 ↓ 4 →	4	11 ↓	7 ↓ 9 →	3	2	4
25 →	5	3	9	8	21 ↓ 6 →	6	28 →	7	3	9	4	5
9 →	8	1	17 ↓	11 ↓ 12 →	9	3	7 ↓ 5 →	1	4	7 ↓ 1 →	1	8 ↓
44 →	2	9	8	6	5	4	7	3	25 ↓ 18 →	7	6	5
	15 ↓ 22 →	6	3	5	7	1	11 ↓	14 ↓ 7 →	7	4 ↓ 11 →	8	3
2 →	2	28 ↓ 1 →	1	3 ↓		22 ↓ 32 →	7	9	8	3	5	6 ↓
23 →	9	7	5	2	5 ↓ 25 →	9	4	5	6	1	11 ↓ 2 →	2
12 →	4	8	15 ↓ 9 →	1	3	5	20 ↓	14 ↓ 3 →	3	8 ↓ 10 →	6	4
	6 ↓ 5 →	2	3	15 ↓ 35 →	2	8	7	9	1	3	5	10 ↓
16 →	1	5	4	6	1 ↓	3 ↓ 14 →	9	5	2 ↓ 5 →	5	3 ↓ 3 →	3
36 →	5	6	8	9	1	3	4	2 →	2	10 →	3	7

	4↓	33↓	17↓	16↓	13↓	9↓				9↓		
30→	4	8	2	6	1	9	2↓	1↓	9→	9	20↓	
	7↓ 17→	2	5	7	3	14↓ 3→	2	1	7↓	9↓ 7→	7	18↓
31→	7	5	1	3	9	6	8↓	3↓ 25→	6	9	8	2
	45↓ 15→	6	9	12↓	20↓ 14→	8	2	3	1	5↓ 7→	3	4
14→	5	9	19↓ 8→	2	6	4↓ 6→	6	18↓	15↓ 10→	1	2	7
25→	6	3	2	9	1	4	27↓ 15→	6	5	4	7↓ 5→	5
4→	4	20↓ 16→	7	1	8	14↓ 15→	4	9	2	16↓ 7→	7	15↓
18→	9	8	1	26→	5	1	2	3	8	7	11↓ 8→	8
18→	8	6	4		21↓ 9→	2	7	17↓	12↓ 18→	9	5	4
8→	2	1	5	24↓ 31→	9	3	8	6	5	5↓ 9→	6	3
6→	1	5	6↓ 33→	2	1	8	6	4	7	5	15↓	11↓
3→	3	23↓ 19→	6	9	4	24↓	22↓ 7→	7	14↓	13↓ 8→	6	2
16→	7	9	14↓ 21→	8	7	1	5	3↓ 21→	7	4	1	9
	3↓ 9→	3	1	5	28→	5	2	3	1	9	8	16↓
15→	3	4	8	9↓	8↓ 10→	4	6	13↓ 6→	6		11↓ 2→	2
	11↓ 39→	6	5	1	8	3	9	7	10↓	11↓ 12→	3	9
7→	6	1	3↓ 8→	8	4↓ 9→	9	27→	4	7	3	8	5
5→	5	3→	3	6→	4	2	13→	2	3	8		

	9↓	13↓		1↓	33↓	18↓	8↓	9↓	6↓	7↓	3↓	8↓
13→	8	5	13↓ 45→	1	5	4	2	9	6	7	3	8
15→	1	6	8	10↓ 12→	4	2	6	17↓	3↓	5↓	4↓	23↓
	5↓ 24→	2	5	6	8	3	5↓ 27→	9	3	5	4	6
5→	5	7↓	26↓ 32→	3	7	9	5	8	18↓	20↓	6↓ 7→	7
	29↓ 23→	7	6	1	9	4↓	10↓	9↓ 30→	7	9	6	8
8→	8	7↓ 5→	5	7↓	11↓ 22→	4	1	9	5	3	13↓ 2→	2
26→	5	7	9	4	1	6→	6	40↓ 15→	6	8	1	21↓
3→	3	27↓ 6→	1	3	2	18↓ 7→	3	4	4↓	20↓ 11→	3	8
14→	4	8	2	7↓ 9→	8	1	25→	5	3	1	9	7
13→	2	1	3	7	11↓ 7→	7	5↓ 14→	7	1	6	13↓ 4→	4
10→	7	3	20↓	7↓ 18→	3	4	5	6	17→	9	6	2
	28↓ 32→	9	7	2	8	6	21↓ 9→	9	6→	4	2	
15→	5	6	3	1	26↓	7↓ 17→	9	8	17↓	8↓ 5→	5	20↓
3→	3	21↓ 40→	2	4	3	7	6	1	9	8	21↓ 5→	5
19→	7	4	8	15↓ 8→	8	1→	1	9↓ 8→	8	12↓ 11→	2	9
17→	8	9	13→	8	5	9↓ 7→	5	2	6↓ 14→	5	3	6
6→	1	5	6↓ 20→	7	9	4	8↓ 17→	3	4	1	9	
13→	4	3	6	33→	1	5	8	4	2	6	7	

	20↓		14↓	4↓	12↓	13↓	14↓	14↓	8↓	9↓		19↓
8→	8	13↓ 42→	1	4	7	2	6	5	8	9	14↓ 7→	7
16→	7	1	8	23↓ 25→	5	3	8	9	3↓	21↓ 11→	3	8
20→	4	3	5	8	28↓ 8→	8	16↓	13↓ 21→	3	9	5	4
10→	1	9	5↓ 15→	6	9	4↓ 8→	5	3	8↓ 7→	1	6	33↓
	24↓	19↓ 39→	1	9	7	4	3	2	8	5	17↓ 8→	8
13→	6	3	4	20↓ 4→	4	7↓ 10→	2	8	9↓ 19→	6	8	5
10→	3	7	16↓ 17→	7	3	1	6	37↓ 3→	3	20↓ 9→	2	7
34→	2	9	4	8	5	6	3↓ 31→	8	6	1	7	9
8→	8	13→	8	5	21↓	17↓ 7→	3	4	16↓ 7→	7	15↓ 4→	4
5→	5	1→	1	36↓ 13→	6	7	14→	1	4	3	6	13↓
	17↓	4↓ 19→	3	5	2	9	6↓ 23→	6	5	9	2	1
7→	3	4	5↓ 28→	8	4	1	6	2	7	22↓ 11→	7	4
5→	5	20↓ 12→	2	1	9	8↓	16↓ 9→	9	9↓ 6→	6	6↓ 8→	8
21→	8	4	3	6	18↓ 25→	2	5	7	1	4	6	20↓
10→	1	9	10↓ 24→	7	4	5	8	2↓ 17→	8	9	1→	1
	9↓ 32→	7	4	9	6	1	3	2	15↓ 3→	3	3↓ 9→	9
6→	6	9↓ 6→	6	3↓ 3→	3	2↓	6↓	4↓ 6→	6	7↓ 7→	3	4
12→	3	9	36→	3	5	2	6	4	9	7	6→	6

	8 ↓		27 ↓	8 ↓		13 ↓	13 ↓	9 ↓	6 ↓	13 ↓	5 ↓	3 ↓
8 →	8	8 ↓ 13 →	8	5	11 ↓ 42 →	9	7	4	6	8	5	3
	15 ↓ 29 →	8	1	3	2	4	6	5	16 ↓ 5 →	5	22 ↓	18 ↓
5 →	5	22 ↓ 9 →	9	8 ↓ 4 →	4	13 ↓	1 ↓	11 ↓ 7 →	7	12 →	5	7
45 →	7	6	4	8	5	3	1	2	9	26 ↓ 13 →	4	9
9 →	3	1	5	19 ↓	3 ↓ 9 →	9	27 ↓ 9 →	9	11 ↓ 8 →	5	1	2
	12 ↓ 4 →	4	19 ↓ 18 →	7	2	1	8	18 ↓ 22 →	6	7	9	3 ↓
27 →	6	9	7	4	1	17 ↓ 33 →	9	7	5	8	3	1
17 →	4	2	8	3	24 ↓ 9 →	2	4	3	2 →	2	24 ↓ 2 →	2
2 →	2	30 →	1	5	3	7	6	8	7 ↓ 9 →	4	5	18 ↓
	41 ↓	13 ↓ 3 →	3	5 ↓ 15 →	7	8	14 ↓	8 ↓ 7 →	7	9 ↓ 10 →	1	9
8 →	2	6	25 ↓ 11 →	5	6	22 ↓ 12 →	4	8	21 ↓ 18 →	4	8	6
11 →	1	4	6	11 ↓ 18 →	8	7	3	21 →	6	5	7	3
24 →	7	3	8	6	2 ↓ 6 →	5	1	15 ↓ 9 →	9	8 ↓ 3 →	3	22 ↓
9 →	9	17 ↓ 40 →	9	4	2	3	6	7	1	8	14 ↓ 6 →	6
16 →	8	5	2	1	8 ↓ 1 →	1	3 ↓ 13 →	8	5	12 ↓ 5 →	3	2
4 →	3	1	3 ↓	12 ↓ 17 →	8	6	3	4 ↓	11 ↓ 16 →	3	4	9
17 →	5	7	1	4	7 ↓	9 ↓	1 ↓ 20 →	4	3	2	6	5
37 →	6	4	2	8	7	9	1	16 →	8	7	1	

	30↓			16↓	20↓	7↓	9↓	19↓	2↓	7↓	11↓	
4→	4	20↓	1↓ 37→	4	1	5	9	6	2	7	3	5↓
22→	7	4	1	3	5	2	16↓ 3→	3	13↓	13↓ 11→	8	3
10→	9	1	11↓ 17→	9	8	12↓ 25→	7	8	1	9	7↓ 2→	2
13→	3	8	2	34→	6	5	1	2	9	4	7	2↓
20→	6	5	9	8↓	21↓ 12→	4	8	8↓ 3→	3	17↓	17↓ 2→	2
3→	1	2	11↓ 17→	8	7	2	5↓ 5→	5	17↓ 12→	5	7	
		25↓ 8→	8	18↓ 32→	9	1	5	3	2	8	4	11↓
	21↓ 23→	7	3	9	4	6↓	15↓	20↓ 26→	7	4	6	9
7→	6	1	20↓ 26→	5	1	6	2	4	8	13↓	10↓ 2→	2
20→	5	8	3	4	19↓	26↓ 13→	4	9	6↓ 14→	5	9	
15→	2	9	4	16↓ 36→	2	3	9	7	6	8	1	34↓
8→	8	18↓ 20→	7	2	5	6	8↓	9↓	1↓	2↓	9→	9
	15↓ 45→	4	6	5	3	9	8	7	1	2	15↓ 8→	8
7→	6	1	18→	9	1	8	17↓ 2→	2	24↓	17↓ 15→	8	7
11→	9	2	11↓	11↓ 8→	8	13↓ 1→	1	1↓ 22→	9	5	7	1
	1↓ 17→	8	5	4	13↓ 22→	3	9	1	5	4	15↓ 2→	2
31→	1	3	6	7	4	8	2	19→	8	2	6	3
				16→	9	2	5	21→	2	6	9	4

	36 ↓	29 ↓	5 ↓	22 ↓	1 ↓	11 ↓	7 ↓	9 ↓	7 ↓		23 ↓	17 ↓
45 →	6	8	3	9	1	4	5	2	7	20 ↓ 15 →	7	8
19 →	3	9	2	5	18 ↓ 14 →	5	2	7	16 ↓ 20 →	6	9	5
9 →	2	7	26 ↓ 12 →	7	3	2	14 ↓	10 ↓ 16 →	1	8	3	4
27 →	4	5	8	1	9	14 ↓ 25 →	9	3	7	2	4	10 ↓
8 →	8	14 ↓ 6 →	6	6 ↓ 32 →	6	2	5	7	8	4	20 ↓ 2 →	2
19 →	7	2	9	1	25 ↓ 5 →	5	17 ↓	8 ↓	6 ↓	11 →	6	5
45 →	1	4	3	5	2	7	9	8	6	7 ↓ 4 →	1	3
13 →	5	8	25 ↓	16 ↓ 9 →	9	7 ↓ 8 →	8	11 ↓	6 ↓ 12 →	7	5	22 ↓
	41 ↓	10 ↓ 19 →	7	5	6	1	8 ↓ 10 →	4	6	15 ↓ 9 →	8	1
39 →	5	3	1	9	8	4	2	7	28 ↓ 9 →	9	5 →	5
21 →	7	4	8	2	24 ↓ 8 →	2	6	7 ↓ 10 →	8	2	28 ↓ 7 →	7
16 →	6	1	9	31 ↓ 8 →	8	18 ↓	17 ↓ 24 →	3	2	4	6	9
11 →	9	2	30 ↓ 24 →	1	2	3	8	4	6	22 ↓ 5 →	5	
8 →	8	31 →	5	6	4	7	9	15 ↓ 22 →	7	6	9	6 ↓
1 →	1	28 →	4	9	7	8	19 ↓ 24 →	2	5	3	8	6
2 →	2	3 ↓ 17 →	6	8	3	4 ↓ 10 →	9	1	9 ↓ 1 →	1	3 ↓	9 ↓
19 →	3	1	8	7	2 ↓ 39 →	3	6	7	9	8	2	4
	9 →	2	7	12 →	2	1	4	5	10 →	4	1	5

	8↓	8↓	14↓		18↓	4↓	14↓	21↓	10↓	9↓	10↓	1↓
13→	2	8	3	13↓ 38→	3	4	5	6	8	9	2	1
6→	6	16→	6	2	8	22↓ 10→	1	7	2	20↓ 7→	7	11↓
		21↓ 32→	5	1	7	9	2	8	7↓ 8→	3	1	4
	34↓ 1→	1	15↓ 3→	3	12↓ 14→	8	6	4↓ 15→	7	8	18↓ 2→	2
27→	1	8	5	7	4	2	20↓ 4→	4	18→	4	9	5
10→	5	2	3	11↓ 13→	6	3	4	24↓	20↓ 6→	5	1	12↓
27→	9	3	7	6	2	6↓ 11→	1	8	2	9↓ 17→	8	9
15→	8	7	20↓ 5→	5	23↓ 25→	4	2	7	3	9	10↓ 3→	3
7→	7	35↓ 6→	6	26→	7	2	8	3	6	8↓ 1→	1	
18→	4	5	9	21↓ 9→	9	30→	5	6	9	8	2	15↓
	6↓ 20→	8	3	7	2		18↓	9↓	8↓	22↓ 12→	4	8
24→	6	7	2	5	4	14↓ 28→	6	7	1	9	3	2
	24↓ 2→	2	19↓ 37→	9	1	6	7	2	4	8	13↓ 5→	5
19→	2	9	8	17↓	11↓ 8→	3	5	22↓ 12→	3	5	4	12↓
35→	6	3	4	8	9	5	19↓ 5→	5	5↓	4↓ 3→	1	2
24→	5	1	7	9	2	4↓ 36→	6	9	2	4	8	7
3→	3	4↓	7↓	5↓	19→	4	5	7	3	2↓	7↓ 3→	3
24→	8	4	7	5		9→	8	1	9→	2	7	

	37 ↓	1 ↓	23 ↓	7 ↓	13 ↓		9 ↓	12 ↓	16 ↓	7 ↓	8 ↓	7 ↓
18 →	3	1	2	7	5	18 ↓ 36 →	9	4	6	7	8	2
8 →	8	13 ↓ 8 →	8	5 ↓ 11 →	8	3	10 ↓ 7 →	5	2	11 ↓	17 ↓ 5 →	5
18 →	1	6	9	2	20 ↓ 33 →	9	8	3	1	5	7	12 ↓
36 →	5	7	4	3	9	6	2	13 ↓ 14 →	7	2	4	1
9 →	9	18 ↓	3 ↓	18 ↓ 1 →	1	9 ↓	14 ↓ 9 →	9	18 →	4	6	8
39 →	7	5	1	3	2	9	8	4	10 ↓	21 ↓	16 ↓ 3 →	3
23 →	4	3	2	6	8	17 ↓ 6 →	6	19 →	9	8	2	5 ↓
	45 ↓ 2 →	2	13 ↓ 9 →	9	29 ↓ 9 →	9	15 ↓	3 ↓ 16 →	1	7	3	5
17 →	4	8	5	3 ↓ 18 →	8	1	6	3	13 ↓ 8 →	2	6	20 ↓
2 →	2	12 ↓ 27 →	6	3	4	5	9	7 ↓ 24 →	6	4	5	9
19 →	8	9	2	21 ↓ 3 →	1	2	27 ↓ 11 →	7	4	10 ↓	1 →	1
10 →	7	3	18 ↓ 16 →	7	9	2 ↓ 6 →	6	1 ↓ 5 →	3	2	10 ↓ 3 →	3
9 →	9	23 ↓ 23 →	3	8	5	2	4	1	9 ↓ 20 →	8	5	7
26 →	3	8	7	6	2	9 →	9	26 ↓ 1 →	1	12 ↓ 3 →	3	1 ↓
16 →	5	9	2		14 ↓	5 ↓ 24 →	7	5	6	3	2	1
9 →	1	2	6	32 →	7	5	1	8	2	9	8 ↓	
10 →	6	4	6 ↓	7 ↓ 6 →	6	3 ↓	9 ↓ 9 →	9	2 ↓	5 ↓ 8 →	8	9 ↓
		37 →	6	7	1	3	9	4	2	5	9 →	9

	25 ↓	35 ↓	7 ↓	9 ↓	5 ↓	12 ↓		30 ↓	18 ↓	16 ↓	7 ↓	7 ↓
30 →	6	2	7	9	5	1	7 ↓ 30 →	8	7	9	5	1
9 →	1	8	18 ↓	20 ↓	15 ↓ 36 →	3	7	9	5	4	2	6
30 →	3	9	2	1	7	8	9 ↓ 12 →	4	6	2	8 ↓	13 ↓
33 →	9	4	7	5	8	18 ↓ 11 →	9	2	15 →	1	8	6
20 →	4	7	1	8	6 →	6	7 ↓ 1 →	1	14 ↓	7 ↓	3 ↓ 3 →	3
21 →	2	5	8	6	12 ↓ 32 →	9	7	6	1	2	3	4
	28 ↓	26 ↓	16 ↓	9 ↓ 5 →	3	2		19 ↓ 8 →	3	5	7 ↓	18 ↓
31 →	8	4	6	3	9	1	17 ↓ 6 →	4	2	14 ↓ 10 →	7	3
23 →	7	9	2	5	6 ↓	27 →	4	9	8	6	27 ↓ 2 →	2
18 →	4	2	5	1	6	8 ↓ 11 →	5	6	13 ↓ 15 →	5	1	9
18 →	9	6	3	8 ↓	10 ↓ 11 →	3	8	28 ↓ 21 →	8	3	6	4
	23 ↓ 5 →	5	15 ↓ 20 →	6	9	5	6 ↓ 8 →	3	5	26 ↓ 7 →	7	12 ↓
5 →	5	31 ↓ 9 →	6	2	1	4 ↓ 6 →	1	5	2 ↓ 17 →	8	4	5
18 →	7	9	2	2 ↓	24 ↓ 31 →	1	5	4	2	3	9	7
27 →	1	8	4	2	9	3	2 →	2	9 →	9	18 ↓	11 ↓
11 →	2	6	3	9 ↓ 3 →	3	5 ↓	16 ↓ 6 →	6	13 ↓ 16 →	6	9	1
11 →	8	3	8 ↓ 28 →	3	5	1	7	8	4	2 ↓ 8 →	5	3
	39 →	5	8	6	7	4	9	22 →	9	2	4	7

	35 ↓	13 ↓	11 ↓	17 ↓	8 ↓	5 ↓	8 ↓	4 ↓			10 ↓	24 ↓
44 →	2	6	3	9	7	5	8	4	12 ↓	14 ↓ 17 →	8	9
25 →	5	4	7	8	1	26 ↓	7 ↓	14 ↓ 17 →	5	6	2	4
12 →	8	3	1	12 ↓	3 ↓ 26 →	6	7	1	4	8	12 ↓ 3 →	3
9 →	9	3 ↓	15 ↓ 6 →	2	3	1	16 ↓ 7 →	4	3	17 ↓ 10 →	9	1
23 →	4	3	7	9	13 ↓ 20 →	8	3	9	19 ↓ 18 →	9	2	7
1 →	1	32 ↓ 26 →	8	1	6	7	4	20 ↓ 14 →	8	5	1	27 ↓
10 →	6	4	21 ↓	10 ↓ 34 →	5	4	9	7	6	3	17 ↓ 9 →	9
	8 ↓ 17 →	1	6	8	2	23 ↓	10 →	8	2	19 ↓ 4 →	1	3
22 →	7	5	8	2	28 ↓ 6 →	6	21 ↓ 25 →	2	3	8	7	5
12 →	1	8	3	1 ↓ 21 →	2	9	7	3	18 ↓ 22 →	7	9	6
	31 ↓ 28 →	2	4	1	7	8	6	22 ↓ 13 →	9	4	7 ↓ 4 →	4
11 →	2	9	22 ↓	5 →	5	14 ↓ 13 →	3	4	6	12 ↓ 7 →	7	12 ↓
15 →	7	3	5	4 ↓ 27 →	6	4	5	7	2	3	12 ↓ 1 →	1
3 →	3	24 ↓ 23 →	9	4	8	2	26 ↓ 25 →	8	1	9	2	5
19 →	4	7	8		14 ↓ 15 →	5	8	2	14 ↓	19 ↓ 9 →	3	6
14 →	8	6	10 ↓	9 ↓ 28 →	6	3	2	1	5	4	7	7 ↓
18 →	1	2	3	4	8	9 ↓ 9 →	9	8 ↓ 16 →	9	7	1 ↓ 1 →	1
27 →	6	9	7	5	24 →	9	7	8	15 →	8	1	6

	7 ↓	23 ↓	14 ↓	14 ↓	5 ↓	14 ↓	1 ↓	8 ↓	2 ↓		7 ↓	16 ↓
45 →	7	9	3	6	5	4	1	8	2	11 ↓ 6 →	4	2
	7 ↓ 15 →	2	5	8	24 ↓ 2 →	2	10 ↓	15 ↓	7 ↓ 14 →	2	3	9
13 →	3	4	6	6 ↓ 30 →	1	8	6	3	7	5	5 ↓ 5 →	5
12 →	4	8	9 ↓ 8 →	6	2	10 ↓ 9 →	4	5	22 ↓ 9 →	4	5	21 ↓
	23 ↓	5 ↓ 7 →	7	6 ↓ 17 →	8	9	12 ↓ 16 →	7	9	14 ↓	14 ↓ 9 →	9
29 →	8	5	2	6	4	1	3	25 ↓ 18 →	3	5	2	8
6 →	6	6 ↓	25 ↓	15 ↓ 9 →	9	7 ↓ 34 →	9	6	5	2	8	4
25 →	9	5	7	4	12 ↓ 5 →	5	25 ↓ 20 →	8	1	7	4	5 ↓
	8 ↓ 40 →	1	8	6	3	2	9	7	4	19 ↓	8 ↓ 5 →	5
6 →	6	30 ↓ 15 →	4	2	9	30 ↓ 11 →	7	4	17 ↓ 10 →	9	1	17 ↓
12 →	2	1	6	3	14 ↓ 13 →	8	5	15 ↓ 25 →	9	3	7	6
	28 ↓ 4 →	4		8 ↓ 32 →	2	5	4	6	8	7	12 ↓ 5 →	5
4 →	1	3	21 ↓ 21 →	8	9	4	14 ↓ 9 →	9	19 ↓	13 ↓ 10 →	8	2
14 →	3	9	2	6 ↓ 19 →	3	7	9	20 ↓ 16 →	2	9	1	4
26 →	7	5	8	6	11 ↓ 33 →	6	5	7	8	4	3	
16 →	2	8	6	2 →	2	5 ↓	6 ↓ 12 →	3	9	5 ↓		12 ↓
6 →	6	1 ↓ 1 →	1	8 ↓ 17 →	6	5	4	2	3 ↓ 5 →	5	8 ↓ 9 →	9
25 →	9	1	4	8	3	13 →	2	8	3	11 →	8	3

	45 ↓	19 ↓	18 ↓		10 ↓	5 ↓	15 ↓	8 ↓	12 ↓	16 ↓		9 ↓
13 →	4	2	7	9 ↓ 32 →	9	5	4	1	7	6	5 ↓ 9 →	9
30 →	8	9	5	7	1	23 →	6	7	3	2	5	
18 →	3	7	6	2	22 ↓	11 ↓ 2 →	2	22 ↓ 10 →	2	8		17 ↓
7 →	6	1	10 ↓	14 ↓ 21 →	1	8	3	9	6 ↓	24 ↓	17 ↓ 9 →	9
9 →	9	30 ↓ 18 →	1	8	6	3	11 ↓ 24 →	6	2	4	5	7
24 →	2	9	4	6	3	15 ↓ 34 →	8	5	4	7	9	1
15 →	7	3	5	10 ↓ 19 →	7	9	1	2	7 ↓ 4 →	1	3	4 ↓
11 →	5	6	9 ↓ 16 →	3	5	6	2	17 ↓ 14 →	5	9	22 ↓ 4 →	4
19 →	1	8	3	7	9 ↓	31 ↓	11 ↓ 14 →	1	2	3	8	11 ↓
	36 ↓ 10 →	4	6	10 ↓ 30 →	7	8	6	9		11 ↓ 7 →	5	2
8 →	8	26 ↓	12 ↓ 20 →	1	2	9	5	3	3 ↓ 15 →	5	9	1
22 →	2	9	8	3	14 ↓ 6 →	6	13 →	4	3	6	15 ↓ 8 →	8
39 →	7	8	4	6	9	5		1 ↓	11 ↓	25 ↓ 8 →	8	8 ↓
6 →	1	5	13 ↓	13 ↓ 8 →	5	3	19 ↓ 18 →	1	7	3	5	2
18 →	9	4	3	2		11 ↓ 8 →	8	13 ↓ 17 →	4	5	2	6
6 →	6	15 ↓ 8 →	2	6	11 ↓ 17 →	6	2	9	6 →	6	6 ↓	
39 →	3	8	7	5	2	1	9	4	15 →	9	6	9 ↓
	8 →	7	1	13 →	9	4			2 →	2	9 →	9

	40 ↓	32 ↓	23 ↓	8 ↓	16 ↓	6 ↓	1 ↓	3 ↓		21 ↓	26 ↓	
38 →	4	8	2	5	9	6	1	3	3 ↓ 10 →	7	3	8 ↓
26 →	6	1	9	3	7	8 ↓	29 ↓	20 ↓ 24 →	3	4	9	8
19 →	3	9	7	19 ↓	18 →	8	4	6	13 ↓ 7 →	1	6	9 ↓
29 →	9	7	5	8	6 ↓	8 ↓ 31 →	1	5	2	9	8	6
3 →	1	2	24 ↓ 34 →	2	6	8	5	9	4	34 ↓	12 ↓ 3 →	3
23 →	8	5	4	6	9 ↓	25 ↓ 3 →	3	7 ↓ 14 →	7	4	3	18 ↓
7 →	7	32 ↓ 26 →	1	3	4	2	9	7	22 ↓ 21 →	8	9	4
13 →	2	8	3	20 ↓ 20 →	5	8	7	7 ↓ 10 →	8	2	5 ↓ 7 →	7
	28 ↓ 18 →	6	9	3	4 ↓ 9 →	9	9 ↓ 19 →	7	1	6	3	2
37 →	2	1	7	8	4	6	9	22 ↓ 20 →	4	9	2	5
9 →	4	5	17 ↓ 5 →	5		13 ↓	9 ↓ 16 →	8	3	5	22 ↓	10 ↓
10 →	1	3	2	4	32 ↓ 28 →	8	9	5	6	11 →	6	5
22 →	6	9	7	13 ↓ 12 →	7	5	25 ↓ 1 →	1	19 ↓	12 →	9	3
7 →	7	30 ↓ 19 →	8	2	9	10 ↓ 9 →	4	2	3	9 →	7	2
10 →	3	7	30 →	3	1	8	5	6	7	10 ↓	18 ↓	10 ↓
13 →	5	8	8 ↓ 18 →	1	6	2	9	11 ↓ 30 →	9	7	6	8
	4 ↓ 23 →	9	3	7	4	7 ↓ 13 →	7	6	13 →	3	8	2
15 →	4	6	5	12 →	5	7	5 →	5		4 →	4	

	12↓	2↓	3↓	31↓	5↓			26↓	8↓	16↓	13↓	15↓
26→	9	2	3	7	5	7↓	4↓ 27→	7	8	2	9	1
2→	2	11↓	4→	4	4↓ 7→	2	4	1	22↓ 19→	9	4	6
3→	1	2	9↓ 12→	6	1	5	14↓ 17→	3	9	5	5→	5
	40↓ 24→	4	9	8	3	15↓ 16→	2	6	8		32↓ 3→	3
11→	6	5	10↓ 5→	5	16↓ 18→	5	3	9	1	8→	8	8↓
3→	3	28→	4	1	6	8	9	15↓ 4→	4	6→	4	2
7→	7	12↓ 6→	6	28↓ 5→	3	2	25↓ 4→	4	6↓	26↓ 11→	6	5
5→	1	4	6↓ 16→	9	7	30→	5	8	6	7	3	1
20→	8	3	5	4	14↓	10↓ 12→	9	3	15↓ 10→	1	9	16↓
33→	9	5	1	6	2	3	7	21→	8	4	2	7
4→	4	5↓	21→	2	8	7	4	21↓ 9→	7	2	15↓ 3→	3
7→	2	5	4↓ 11→	7	4	34↓	5↓ 9→	9	3↓ 10→	3	1	6
	22↓	22↓ 4→	4	5↓	1↓ 35→	7	5	4	2	9	8	5↓
11→	9	2	8↓ 13→	4	1	8	15↓ 9→	8	1	9↓ 9→	6	3
15→	5	7	2	1	18↓ 14→	9	5	7↓	16↓ 2→	2	1↓ 2→	2
17→	7	4	6	7↓ 31→	8	3	4	7	2	6	1	7↓
4→	1	3	8↓ 13→	4	1	2	6	8↓ 10→	9	1	9↓ 5→	5
	31→	6	8	3	9	5	13→	8	5	11→	9	2

	1 ↓	20 ↓	11 ↓	2 ↓	26 ↓		21 ↓	4 ↓	15 ↓	11 ↓	10 ↓	10 ↓
18 →	1	4	3	2	8	14 ↓ 34 →	8	4	5	2	6	9
	13 →	5	8	20 ↓ 20 →	5	6	9	1 ↓ 20 →	7	9	3	1
	33 ↓ 8 →	8	31 ↓ 25 →	2	7	8	4	1	3	1 →	1	11 ↓
33 →	7	3	8	9	6	5 ↓	13 ↓	27 ↓		10 ↓	3 →	3
8 →	8	7 →	2	5	21 ↓ 9 →	5	1	3	16 ↓ 4 →	4	21 ↓ 2 →	2
6 →	6	21 ↓ 16 →	5	4	7	13 ↓ 34 →	4	2	8	6	9	5
10 →	4	5	1	27 →	1	4	8	9	5	8 ↓ 8 →	7	1
16 →	3	7	6	12 →	3	9	11 ↓ 22 →	6	3	8	5	
15 →	5	1	9	18 ↓ 2 →	2	13 ↓ 8 →	1	7	19 ↓	25 ↓	12 ↓	8 ↓
	7 ↓ 6 →	6	20 ↓ 22 →	3	8	5	6	27 →	8	9	4	6
22 →	7	2	8	5	20 ↓ 6 →	2	4	4 ↓ 17 →	5	3	7	2
	27 ↓	18 ↓ 19 →	5	1	7	6	12 ↓ 15 →	4	3	7	1	9 ↓
28 →	1	6	4	9	8	9 →	9	28 ↓ 8 →	2	6	25 ↓ 4 →	4
16 →	8	5	3	10 ↓ 2 →	2	2 ↓ 13 →	3	9	1	1 ↓ 11 →	6	5
10 →	3	7	9 ↓ 9 →	4	3	2	8 ↓ 8 →	8	3 ↓ 8 →	1	7	11 ↓
5 →	5	12 ↓ 11 →	5	6	11 ↓	8 ↓ 10 →	1	6	3	17 ↓ 12 →	5	7
18 →	6	9	3	7 ↓ 17 →	2	3	7	5	2 ↓ 15 →	8	3	4
29 →	4	3	1	7	9	5		15 →	2	9	4	

	6 ↓	30 ↓	13 ↓		14 ↓	15 ↓	9 ↓	4 ↓	17 ↓		6 ↓	13 ↓
10 →	4	1	5	16 ↓ 22 →	3	5	8	4	2	10 ↓ 11 →	5	6
37 →	2	7	8	4	6	9	1	10 ↓ 17 →	6	3	1	7
	15 ↓ 5 →	5	18 ↓ 12 →	6	5	1	3 ↓ 17 →	1	9	7	2 ↓	
20 →	3	9	7	1	2 ↓	7 ↓ 8 →	2	6		28 ↓ 2 →	2	11 ↓
36 →	7	8	6	5	2	4	1	3	11 ↓ 5 →	5	8 →	8
5 →	5	23 ↓ 5 →	5	31 ↓	11 ↓ 3 →	3	8 ↓	17 ↓ 9 →	1	8	7 ↓ 2 →	2
	7 ↓ 7 →	7	11 ↓ 10 →	6	4	11 ↓ 34 →	8	7	5	9	4	1
23 →	1	6	4	3	7	2	18 ↓ 12 →	1	2	6	3	19 ↓
24 →	6	2	7	9	2 ↓ 22 →	9	6	4	3	29 ↓	4 ↓ 7 →	7
	28 ↓ 8 →	8	24 ↓ 7 →	5	2	19 ↓ 12 →	7	5	4 ↓ 12 →	2	4	6
9 →	9	11 ↓ 13 →	5	8	9 ↓ 11 →	8	3	6 ↓ 9 →	4	5	22 ↓ 5 →	5
13 →	3	2	8	13 ↓ 16 →	3	5	2	6	12 ↓ 17 →	7	9	1
35 →	7	9	4	8	1	6	19 ↓	19 ↓ 12 →	3	1	8	
1 →	1	12 ↓ 8 →	1	2	5	20 ↓ 28 →	2	4	9	8	5	23 ↓
22 →	8	5	6	3	14 ↓ 16 →	4	3	9	3 ↓ 6 →	6	13 ↓ 4 →	4
	4 →	4	10 ↓	6 ↓ 19 →	2	7	1	6	3	7 ↓ 9 →	7	2
	4 ↓ 28 →	1	3	6	4	9	5	1 ↓	21 →	7	6	8
13 →	4	2	7	8 →	8	9 →	8	1			9 →	9

	5 ↓	22 ↓	15 ↓	14 ↓		7 ↓	1 ↓	21 ↓	16 ↓	13 ↓	2 ↓	12 ↓
13 →	5	4	1	3	5 ↓ 32 →	5	1	8	7	6	2	3
	32 ↓ 25 →	7	6	9	1	2	16 ↓ 19 →	6	9	4	8 ↓ 9 →	9
22 →	5	3	8	2	4	26 ↓ 8 →	1	7	14 ↓ 9 →	3	6	12 ↓
14 →	6	8	35 ↓	16 ↓	8 ↓ 9 →	4	5	4 ↓ 4 →	4	16 ↓ 5 →	2	3
8 →	8	38 →	5	6	8	2	3	4	1	9	12 ↓ 4 →	4
9 →	9	16 →	7	9	16 →	9	7	6 ↓ 27 →	9	7	6	5
4 →	4	36 ↓ 10 →	9	1	14 ↓ 1 →	1	10 ↓ 4 →	4	14 ↓	9 ↓ 1 →	1	8 ↓
	22 ↓ 11 →	8	3	19 ↓ 44 →	9	3	6	2	8	4	5	7
36 →	8	5	1	9	2	7	4	6 →	1	5	28 ↓ 1 →	1
27 →	9	2	6	7	3		8 ↓	18 ↓ 5 →	5	9 ↓ 3 →	3	
19 →	5	7	4	3	9 ↓	8 ↓ 11 →	8	3	13 ↓ 12 →	3	9	9 ↓
	6 →	6	33 ↓	17 →	9	8	11 ↓ 23 →	1	2	6	5	9
	21 ↓ 13 →	4	9	13 ↓		19 →	6	5	8	21 ↓ 4 →	4	7 ↓
16 →	7	1	3	5	28 ↓	15 ↓ 32 →	5	9	3	2	7	6
27 →	1	3	5	2	9	7		7 ↓	3 ↓ 4 →	4	20 ↓ 1 →	1
6 →	6	3 ↓ 20 →	2	6	4	8	13 ↓ 17 →	2	3	7	5	
12 →	4	2	6	8 →	8	6 ↓ 9 →	5	4	17 →	8	9	5 ↓
12 →	3	1	8	22 →	7	6	8	1		11 →	6	5

	41↓	24↓	21↓	6↓	2↓	13↓		18↓	18↓		4↓	
27→	5	7	8	4	2	1	23↓ 7→	3	4	4→	4	19↓
20→	6	3	9	2	24↓ 15→	3	6	1	5	1↓	9→	9
20→	7	9	4	27↓ 32→	6	9	4	5	7	1	11↓ 4→	4
6→	2	4	12↓ 10→	1	9	17→	8	7	2	22↓ 7→	6	1
26→	9	1	3	8	5	15↓ 7→	5	2	18↓ 15→	8	2	5
1→	1	18↓ 14→	2	7	4	1	7↓	18→	8	7	3	
20→	3	4	7	6	13↓ 15→	8	7	15↓ 5→	3	2	21↓	10↓
10→	8	2	17↓ 12→	5	1	6	8↓ 28→	9	7	1	6	5
	45↓ 13→	5	8	9↓ 4→	4	7→	1	6	16↓ 15→	4	8	3
28→	3	6	7	4	8	24↓ 7→	7	13↓ 2→	2	6↓ 7→	5	2
17→	9	1	2	5	3→	3	9↓ 14→	1	5	6	2	25↓
7→	7		29↓		9↓ 20→	1	3	7	9	13↓	5↓ 2→	2
1→	1	6↓ 5→	5	9↓ 26→	9	8	4	5	23↓ 15→	7	3	5
24→	5	6	9	4	9↓ 7→	5	2	19↓ 18→	9	1	2	6
2→	2	15↓ 22→	4	2	9	7	8↓ 8→	2	1	5	13↓ 8→	8
20→	4	6	7	3		6↓ 15→	7	3	5	10↓ 10→	6	4
11→	8	2	1	5↓	4↓ 34→	4	1	9	8	7	5	4↓
27→	6	7	3	5	4	2	5→	5	9→	3	2	4

		34 ↓	13 ↓	3 ↓	1 ↓	24 ↓		30 ↓	10 ↓	10 ↓	1 ↓	8 ↓
	39 ↓ 23 →	8	9	3	1	2	13 ↓ 23 →	5	7	2	1	8
12 →	2	9	1	9 ↓	25 →	4	3	9	1	8		15 ↓
24 →	5	7	3	9	18 ↓ 14 →	5	1	6	2	31 ↓	19 ↓ 9 →	9
15 →	9	6	5 ↓	18 ↓ 24 →	1	6	9	8	29 ↓ 16 →	4	7	5
34 →	1	4	5	9	8	7	9 ↓ 15 →	2	4	5	3	1
7 →	7	21 ↓	20 ↓ 8 →	2	6	11 ↓ 7 →	7	10 →	3	6	1	4 ↓
39 →	4	9	8	7	3	6	2	23 ↓ 24 →	5	7	8	4
20 →	8	7	5	10 ↓	13 ↓ 5 →	5	21 ↓ 22 →	6	7	9	24 ↓	
24 →	3	5	6	1	9	13 →	4	8	1	3 →	3	17 ↓
	20 ↓	25 ↓ 7 →	1	2	4	14 ↓ 21 →	5	7	9	17 ↓ 11 →	9	2
16 →	7	9	16 ↓ 7 →	7	16 ↓ 12 →	1	9	2	16 ↓ 19 →	6	8	5
17 →	5	8	4	12 ↓ 17 →	9	5	3	25 ↓ 10 →	1	2	4	3
30 →	4	2	3	6	7	8	10 ↓ 19 →	2	8	9	25 ↓ 7 →	7
23 →	3	6	9	5	3 ↓	19 ↓ 13 →	2	8	3	5 →	5	14 ↓
1 →	1		14 ↓ 27 →	1	3	5	8	6	4	3 ↓ 8 →	3	5
	11 ↓	11 ↓ 8 →	8	3 ↓	10 ↓ 2 →	2	7 ↓ 9 →	9	8 ↓ 14 →	3	4	7
32 →	2	6	5	3	1	8	7	9 ↓ 7 →	7	4 ↓ 8 →	6	2
15 →	9	5	1	13 →	9	4	21 →	9	1	4	7	

	7↓	12↓	17↓	12↓	5↓	1↓	17↓		16↓	3↓	9↓	35↓
33→	7	6	5	4	2	1	8	7↓ 14→	2	3	1	8
	40↓ 14→	2	1	8	3	19→	9	7	3	17↓ 13→	8	5
13→	9	1	3	12↓		12↓	7↓	11↓ 9→	5	4	9→	9
20→	4	3	8	5	14↓ 34→	4	7	8	6	9	4↓ 6→	6
1→	1	3↓	22↓ 12→	1	8	3	11↓ 3→	3	7↓ 14→	3	4	7
42→	7	3	9	6	4	5	8	25↓ 5→	4	1	7↓	
8→	8	2→	2	28↓ 2→	2	11↓ 11→	1	7	3	25↓ 6→	6	25↓
6→	6	25↓ 12→	5	7	4↓ 19→	8	2	9	9↓ 16→	7	1	8
28→	5	1	6	9	4	3	22↓ 20→	3	9	8	2↓ 5→	5
	31↓ 9→	9	16↓ 8→	8	29↓	14↓ 10→	4	6	20↓ 16→	5	2	9
35→	7	2	3	4	5	6	8	14↓ 13→	9	4	10↓ 3→	3
13→	1	3	9	38→	6	8	9	7	4	1	3	3↓
18→	8	6	4	5↓ 9→	9	18↓ 6→	1	3	2	18↓ 8→	5	3
10→	6	4	15→	5	1	9	10↓ 20→	4	5	9	2	14↓
9→	9	6↓	12↓	11↓ 12→	8	3	1	14↓	5↓ 7→	7	8→	8
	7↓ 18→	4	8	6	13↓ 21→	6	7	5	1	2	13↓ 6→	6
19→	7	2	1	5	4	7↓ 14→	2	8	4	4→	4	7↓
		3→	3	16→	9	7	1→	1		16→	9	7

	31↓	16↓	19↓	8↓		12↓	30↓	14↓		17↓	15↓	4↓
20→	1	5	6	8	16↓ 14→	4	3	7	18→	5	9	4
15→	9	4	2	14↓ 19→	3	8	6	2	18↓ 7→	4	3	1↓
30→	6	7	3	5	9	20↓ 32→	9	5	7	8	2	1
3→	3	19↓ 28→	8	9	4	2	5	9↓ 8→	8	5↓ 1→	1	15↓
15→	8	7	18↓	14↓	18↓ 24→	6	7	4	2	5	5→	5
29→	4	3	8	1	6	7	10↓ 6→	5	1	1↓	20↓ 2→	2
	13↓ 30→	9	1	6	7	5	2	22↓	2↓ 11→	1	2	8
7→	7	31↓ 14→	2	7	5	11→	8	1	2	12↓ 5→	5	10↓
13→	4	2	7	13↓			13↓ 3→	3	16↓ 9→	3	4	2
10→	2	8	7→	7	7↓	5↓ 35→	4	7	6	1	9	8
	28↓ 5→	5	17↓ 32→	4	1	5	3	9	2	8	21↓	6↓
21→	3	1	9	2	6	22↓ 16→	6	2	8	22↓ 12→	9	3
16→	2	6	8	11↓	12↓ 3→	3	4↓		29↓ 12→	4	7	1
13→	4	9	21↓ 21→	9	7	1	4	5↓ 18→	5	8	3	2
5→	5	15↓ 12→	1	2	5	4	10↓ 17→	5	9	1	2	
14→	1	4	9		11↓ 10→	6	4	8↓ 8→	2	6	10↓	
12→	7	2	3	5↓ 39→	9	8	1	5	7	3	6	9↓
30→	6	9	8	5	2	14→	5	3	6	13→	4	9

	6 ↓	12 ↓		16 ↓	5 ↓	2 ↓	24 ↓	20 ↓	13 ↓		5 ↓	27 ↓
15 →	6	9	11 ↓ 27 →	1	3	2	7	6	8	11 ↓ 9 →	5	4
	21 ↓ 15 →	1	8	4	2	21 ↓ 28 →	8	9	5	6	2 ↓ 8 →	8
14 →	4	2	3	5	21 ↓ 17 →	3	9	5	9 ↓ 14 →	3	2	9
3 →	3	30 ↓	2 ↓ 20 →	6	5	9	16 ↓	4 ↓ 3 →	1	2	9 ↓ 6 →	6
14 →	8	4	2	17 ↓ 29 →	9	7	3	4	6	12 ↓ 2 →	2	9 ↓
9 →	6	3	17 →	9	1	2	5	9 ↓ 26 →	2	8	7	9
	9 ↓ 5 →	5	18 ↓ 7 →	3	4	24 ↓ 13 →	8	5	16 ↓ 3 →	3		16 ↓
29 →	6	7	5	1	2	8	7 →	4	2	1	14 ↓ 8 →	8
17 →	3	2	8	4	24 ↓ 9 →	9	12 ↓	11 ↓ 8 →	8	9 ↓ 16 →	9	7
	3 ↓ 10 →	9	1	27 ↓ 36 →	7	4	2	3	6	8	5	1
2 →	2	14 ↓ 27 →	4	6	5	3	1	8	18 ↓ 1 →	1	6 ↓	18 ↓
10 →	1	9	20 ↓ 10 →	1	9	10 ↓ 9 →	9	18 ↓ 2 →	2	1 ↓ 14 →	6	8
	24 ↓ 27 →	5	7	8	3	4	11 →	4	6	1	23 ↓ 9 →	9
8 →	8	16 ↓ 7 →	4	3	19 ↓ 6 →	6	19 ↓ 6 →	5	1	5 →	4	1
28 →	3	7	1	9	8	13 ↓ 20 →	8	3	9	15 ↓ 9 →	9	13 ↓
12 →	1	9	2	13 ↓ 24 →	2	9	7	6	14 ↓ 24 →	8	7	9
5 →	5	6 ↓ 26 →	6	8	5	3	4	9 ↓ 18 →	6	5	3	4
13 →	7	6	10 →	5	4	1	19 →	9	8	2		

	34↓	8↓	16↓		9↓	13↓	9↓	8↓		30↓	16↓	14↓
18→	9	8	1	17↓ 19→	1	3	7	8	22↓ 22→	9	6	7
2→	2	16↓ 28→	5	7	8	6	2	5↓ 20→	8	4	3	5
18→	3	8	6	1	6↓ 4→	4	15↓ 19→	5	4	1	7	2
29→	8	2	4	9	6	13↓ 1→	1	8↓ 12→	9	3	5↓	17↓
7→	1	6	13↓	18↓	11↓ 37→	4	3	8	1	7	5	9
5→	5	22↓ 28→	4	2	7	9	6	21↓	21↓ 6→	6	17↓ 6→	6
30→	6	5	9	7	3	2↓ 22→	5	9	8	5↓ 5→	3	2
	39↓ 9→	9	15↓ 11→	8	1	2	11↓ 15→	1	7	5	2	25↓
13→	7	3	2	1	17↓	13↓ 12→	2	4	6	9↓ 13→	4	9
11→	2	1	8	27↓ 23→	3	4	9	7	13↓ 15→	1	8	6
39→	8	4	5	9	6	7	11↓	5↓ 17→	9	8	22↓ 2→	2
3→	3	14↓	5↓ 27→	3	7	2	6	5	4	17↓ 7→	2	5
19→	4	3	5	6	1	15↓ 4→	4	15↓	15↓ 20→	8	9	3
7→	6	1	17↓ 2→	2	8↓ 30→	9	1	2	5	6	7	5↓
34→	9	8	1	7	3	6	25→	7	6	3	4	5
	10↓ 8→	2	6	5→	5	10↓	7↓ 10→	6	4	10↓		9↓
6→	6	8↓ 7→	7	5↓	10→	3	7	1↓	3↓ 6→	6	6↓ 2→	2
20→	4	8	3	5	7→	7	21→	1	3	4	6	7

	30↓	2↓	8↓	8↓	20↓	11↓	6↓		13↓	12↓	15↓	
41→	7	2	8	5	9	4	6	20↓ 11→	1	4	6	16↓
2→	2	4↓	24↓ 8→	3	4	1	26↓ 31→	5	3	8	9	6
16→	5	4	7	8↓ 26→	1	6	2	8	9	30↓	11↓ 2→	2
6→	6	20↓ 19→	8	5	6	9↓ 11→	7	4	11→	4	6	1
20→	9	7	3	1	9↓ 17→	5	9	3	15→	6	2	7
33→	1	3	6	2	9	4	8	14↓	8↓ 10→	7	3	30↓
	24↓ 2→	2	14↓	23↓	9↓	4↓	12↓ 14→	5	8	1	5→	5
43→	7	8	5	1	6	4	3	9	24↓ 9→	9	7→	7
6→	6	14→	2	9	3	7↓ 9→	9	6↓ 9→	6	3	23↓ 9→	9
3→	3	18↓ 7→	1	6	14↓ 2→	2	11↓ 10→	6	4	4→	3	1
32→	8	1	6	3	2	5	7	5↓ 5→	5	22↓ 10→	8	2
	26↓ 6→	6	9→	4	5	16↓ 34→	4	2	9	8	5	6
6→	2	4	16↓	15↓ 8→	7	1	19↓ 3→	3	14↓ 8→	1	7	12↓
17→	3	7	6	1	7↓ 15→	9	6	5↓ 8→	2	6	3→	3
9→	9	15↓ 44→	2	9	3	6	8	5	4	7	9↓ 5→	5
33→	7	9	8	5	4	9↓ 5→	5	14↓ 1→	1	11↓ 11→	7	4
9→	5	4	3↓	8↓	1↓ 5→	5	7↓ 21→	9	7	3	2	8↓
	30→	2	3	8	1	4	7	5	8→	8	8→	8

	45↓	17↓	11↓	3↓	2↓	6↓		19↓	10↓	4↓	17↓	
28→	7	9	6	3	2	1	1↓ 28→	9	7	4	8	8↓
11→	4	2	5	24↓	22↓ 11→	5	1	2	3	12↓ 14→	6	8
7→	1	6	14↓ 17→	8	9	5↓	8↓ 8→	8	12↓ 12→	9	3	9↓
2→	2	36↓ 18→	4	2	6	5	1	9→	6	3	26↓ 9→	9
24→	3	8	1	5	7	27↓ 7→	7	16↓ 1→	1	1→	1	19↓
22→	6	5	2	9	9↓ 1→	1	12↓ 14→	9	5	6↓ 15→	9	6
19→	8	4	7	13↓ 22→	8	6	5	3	16↓ 17→	6	4	7
14→	5	9	26↓ 31→	2	1	9	7	4	8	8→	5	3
28→	9	7	8	4	14↓ 4→	4	8↓	14↓ 5→	5	5↓ 8→	7	1
	45→	2	4	1	9	7	8	6	3	5	26↓ 2→	2
	6↓ 15→	1	3	6	5	2↓	10↓ 5→	5		31↓ 7→	7	13↓
5→	5	5→	5	7↓	4↓ 11→	2	6	3	11→	6	3	2
1→	1	13→	6	3	4	14↓ 1→	1	8↓	7→	1	2	4
	15↓	21↓	6↓ 4→	4	15↓ 18→	8	3	7	19↓ 24→	8	9	7
11→	4	1	6	6↓ 15→	9	6	2↓ 23→	1	8	9	5	7↓
17→	8	9	10↓ 10→	4	6	13↓ 2→	2	13↓ 6→	2	4	6↓ 7→	7
12→	1	6	3	2	5↓ 6→	6	23→	5	9	3	6	3↓
14→	2	5	7	12→	5	7	8→	8			3→	3

	41↓		7↓	13↓	14↓	8↓	16↓	8↓	7↓	5↓		8↓
5→	5	9↓ 44→	7	4	9	2	3	8	6	5	18↓ 8→	8
5→	3	2	15↓ 15→	1	3	6	5	6↓ 1→	1	3↓ 2→	2	28↓
26→	8	7	4	5	2	12↓ 14→	8	6	20↓ 10→	1	5	4
2→	2	6↓ 9→	6	3	20↓ 1→	1		22→	9	2	4	7
20→	9	6	5	14↓ 11→	7	4	12↓	5↓ 7→	7	16↓ 15→	7	8
6→	6	6↓	20↓ 37→	6	8	2	3	5	4	9	23↓ 6→	6
39→	7	6	3	8	1	5	9	8↓	2↓ 16→	7	6	3
1→	1	8↓ 5→	5	17↓ 4→	4	17↓	6↓ 7→	5	2	24↓ 1→	1	7↓
	33↓ 18→	6	4	8	20↓ 8→	4	1	3	36↓ 17→	7	9	1
35→	1	2	8	9	3	7	5	6↓ 16→	2	5	3	6
2→	2	30↓	2↓	4↓ 13→	7	6	8↓ 16→	1	8	3	4	15↓
23→	5	9	2	3	4	30↓ 23→	3	5	6	9	27↓ 4→	4
9→	3	6	14↓ 14→	1	6	2	5	1↓ 7→	7	3↓ 10→	4	6
12→	7	1	4		15↓ 7→	7	24↓ 22→	1	4	3	9	5
15→	9	4	2	15→	5	8	2	5↓ 9→	9	16↓ 8→	8	22↓
13→	6	2	5	19→	1	4	9	5	10↓ 18→	7	6	5
	7↓ 11→	8	3	8↓ 18→	3	9	6	8↓ 10→	1	9	5↓ 8→	8
7→	7		14→	8	6	24→	7	8	9	14→	5	9

www.ingramcontent.com/pod-product-compliance
Lightning Source LLC
Chambersburg PA
CBHW051355150726
48000CB00003B/1198

* 9 7 9 8 6 0 6 4 0 1 6 7 3 *